love & light
Susan 🖤

Living In The Light

A Divine Perspective and Guide to Living a Peaceful Life

WRITTEN BY AND THROUGH

Susan Newton

Copyright © 2011 Susan Newton

All rights reserved. No part of this book may be used or reproduced by any means, graphic, electronic, or mechanical, including photocopying, recording, taping or by any information storage retrieval system without the written permission of the publisher except in the case of brief quotations embodied in critical articles and reviews.

Balboa Press books may be ordered through booksellers or by contacting:

Balboa Press
A Division of Hay House
1663 Liberty Drive
Bloomington, IN 47403
www.balboapress.com
1-(877) 407-4847

Because of the dynamic nature of the Internet, any web addresses or links contained in this book may have changed since publication and may no longer be valid. The views expressed in this work are solely those of the author and do not necessarily reflect the views of the publisher, and the publisher hereby disclaims any responsibility for them.

The author of this book does not dispense medical advice or prescribe the use of any technique as a form of treatment for physical, emotional, or medical problems without the advice of a physician, either directly or indirectly. The intent of the author is only to offer information of a general nature to help you in your quest for emotional and spiritual well-being. In the event you use any of the information in this book for yourself, which is your constitutional right, the author and the publisher assume no responsibility for your actions.

ISBN: 978-1-4525-3438-1 (sc)
ISBN: 978-1-4525-3440-4 (hc)
ISBN: 978-1-4525-3439-8 (e)

Library of Congress Control Number: 2011905963

Any people depicted in stock imagery provided by Thinkstock are models, and such images are being used for illustrative purposes only.
Certain stock imagery © Thinkstock.

Print information available on the last page.

Balboa Press rev. date: 3/12/2015

Thank you to Deron & Nicole Klatte of Klatte Photography for the beautiful Photographs of Chris and I. Thank you to all those who contributed financially.

Contents

Forward ix
Preface xi

The Basic Construct 1
The Choice for Personal Shift 5
Taking the High Road 9
Forgiveness: Letting go of Right & Wrong 15
Does This Serve My Highest Good 19
The Commitment of 100% Responsibility 23
The Commitment of 100% Truth 27
The Commitment of 100% Forgiveness 31
The Commitment of Observation 35
What is Unconditional Love 39
Finding Peace in the Pain 43
Communication or Confrontation 47
Perception and Opinion 55
Acceptance or Avoidance 57
Discernment or Judgment 61
Interaction or Reaction 65
Was it really meant to be? 69
Identify the Issue…Focus on the Solution 73
Live In The Light 77
Choose It-Become It-Enjoy It-Love It 79

Thank you 81
Additional Channelings 83
Acknowledgments 101
Special Support Thank You's 107

Forward

I would like to say thank you to all of the beautiful people in my life that have assisted me as I have journeyed! My biological parents who brought me into the world, my parents and family who adopted me and raised me as their own, my children, my partners, my friends, my clients, teachers, authors, and everyone that I have come into contact with have all contributed greatly to my life journey. I am so grateful for all that I have experienced. I didn't always know how to be grateful for the wisdom that can be found in every circumstance, but I know now that there is truly a gift in every experience. All you have to do is look for it. Of course that sounds easy enough to do, and as we all know it can be a bit more challenging to actually achieve that goal. That's why I am excited to share the information and wisdom in this book with everyone who is ready to read it and implement it into their lives! It's my intention to share a user friendly way for people to make positive changes in their lives that will allow them to experience a more peaceful and joyful life experience. When you make a change you get a change. All that is required to make a change is for you to choose to do it! It really is that simple. I hope that you enjoy the book and that you are able to see the results of your choices in your everyday lives and the lives of all those around you!!

Preface

While I am the author of this book, I'd like to take this opportunity to clarify how some of the information in this book was written. I am a Medium and Interactive Verbal Channel and many of the teachings in this book were given to me by Spirit, as I have gone through experiences in my life and asked for guidance. There are Channelings written in this book to go along with my perceptions of the wisdom that I have learned from Spirit and other spiritual teachers that I have followed. There are many people at this time who are listening and sharing from their perspective, and I am grateful to them all! The more who share, the more insights and wisdoms will be received and given. It is indicated in the text where a Channeling is being shared through me. When I allow for this information to enter, I always clarify as follows: "It is with purity of intention and unconditional Love that I request and receive Divine and Pure wisdom to and through my Higher Self, that will serve the highest good of myself and all that is." I call upon The Pleiadian Emissaries of Light, The Arch Angelic League of Light, The Ascended Masters from The City of Light, and the Spirit Guides and Ancestors to share with me their unconditionally loving Divine Perspective. I am always grateful for the opportunity to do this work and share it with others in a way that we can all benefit from! We are all one and are in this world together for a reason. Let's make the best of it together...One For All & All For One!!! :)

The Basic Construct

The basic construct is a way of life! It's a choice to implement some simplistic concepts into your everyday life on a minute by minute experience by experience basis. It requires you to make a choice to lead your life in an honest loving yet empowered way and then to remain committed to doing it on a regular basis. We live in a world that is filled with people; Spirits in Human Form, as spirit refers to us. We now know, thanks to all of the research that has already been done that we are all different parts of the same vibration. There are many wonderful resources on Quantum Physics available to expand on this knowledge.

Keeping in mind that we are All One, it makes sense then that each individual person's thoughts, words, behaviors, feelings, and actions have an impact on the collective consciousness that we are all a part of! This is where the Divine Perspective begins. It would be in everyone's best interest to have as many people as possible choosing to interact in an unconditionally loving and honest way. A way that would have you taking responsibility for your life and all that you are experiencing in it! Of course this isn't a new concept, there are many gifted teachers out there teaching and sharing the same thing in their own way. The way that I see it is that the more who are sharing it the more opportunities there will be for more to hear it! I have enclosed a book list of all the authors whom I have enjoyed reading so that you too can enjoy the wisdom from many different yet similar perspectives!!

So, The Basic Construct is a way of life that involves choosing to take 100% responsibility for your thoughts, words, behaviors, feelings, and actions and the experiences in your life; being 100% honest; learning to be 100% forgiving; learning to observe what you and others are choosing; being unconditionally loving, communicating, discerning, and interacting with your life circumstances and experiences. It is your relationship to everything that determines how you journey through your life. It is a choice to know that your life is happening for you and by you rather than happening to you! Choose not to be the victim; rather choose to be empowered by the knowledge that you always have a choice to find the "GIFT" in your experiences. Really when you think about it, what joy could possibly come from looking at the glass that is ½ empty, especially when we know that we draw to us more of what we are putting out there!

I know that committing 100% to anything sounds a little daunting and could be misconstrued as being limiting to your life experience rather than enhancing it. Keep in mind that the whole premise of this concept is founded in universal principals that are to be applied to where ever you are in the moment, allowing for presence to occur. In other words, the intention is for people to choose on their own to function from a more "light filled / positive" place. Being 100% honest and responsible is subjective and always relative to what you know to be true in that moment. Everyone's perceptions are based on their experiences with their past circumstances in this life as well as past lives. Their ability to be honest and take responsibility allows you to look and observe where you are and make changes when necessary. Living in the Light is simply a construct that can be applied to everything in anyone's life no matter where they are or what their "truth" is in that moment. The commitment is to allow for expansion to occur from wherever you are through the realization that you are only limited if you choose to be. As you allow yourself to "BE" where you are, you empower yourself to move forward in a different way. Truth and responsibility create presence and presence allows for growth and evolution.

So let's learn together how to create positive shifts in our perceptions of our life experiences and choose to be committed to make it happen. I have a t-shirt that says, "Meet Me on the Sunny Side of the Street," what a great motto to live by. This doesn't mean that you aren't going to feel like _____ sometimes! It means that instead of sitting in the _____, you'll find a way to move through it, and out of it, allowing for resolution of the circumstance and forward movement toward a desired solution. It really is just a choice and a commitment to make some small changes in your way of thinking, feeling, acting, and behaving that allow for significant changes to occur in your life, as well as the lives of others! Little by little, step by step, day by day, choice by choice, change by change we will get there together!

Channeling through Susan: We are here and we are excited to be a part of this document. Of course there is much wisdom to be shared with those who are ready to listen. We are very grateful for the opportunity to bring these principles forward in a way that many will resonate with. Of course your world at this time is going through great shifts and changes that are providing opportunities for "Spiritual Growth," as you call it! It is our intention as we unite with you through this writing to experience unconditional love together in a very clear way for all to experience. Peace is always our intention and your openness to view things from a "new" perspective will allow for many great changes to occur. We are honored to be discussing this with you at this time! We love you so much

The Choice for Personal Shift

I would like to share some of my personal life experiences at this time, as this book is a direct result of my interactions with them. I am often asked the question, "Have I always been like this"? The answer to that is a resounding NO! Up until I was in my thirties, I had no knowledge or understanding of what "spirituality" meant. I had been raised in a religious setting that did not encompass the spirit world the way I know it now. I remember thinking quite clearly that many things didn't make sense to me and that often time's people who were supposed to be "good Christians" seemed to be not very nice people. I know that I share in many others view of this topic and I believe that it is changing rapidly now more than ever.

I remember coming to a place in my life that stopped me in my tracks and I literally asked the question out loud through tears, "Why does this keep happening to me?" As soon as the words exited my lips, a shift occurred that changed my life forever. In that split second, I realized that I was the one making the choices for myself and that if I wanted to experience something else, I was the only one responsible for making a different choice. This realization shifted my perception on everything. I began to understand that I had been functioning as though life was happening to me rather than for me. I had been blaming others for "unpleasant" experiences in my life and reacting, rather than taking responsibility for choosing who and what I interacted with. It was an empowering shift that occurred as I look back on it, but at the time it didn't feel that way. I made a choice in that moment to co-create a personal shift by looking at my life as though I were responsible for all of it. I began to read and go to events and workshops that would allow me to become more of what I was capable of. The more I learned, the more I found to learn. Over the course of the next ten years many different shifts and experiences occurred, some more enjoyable than others, but all an important part of my growth.

For me the choice to look at things differently opened my intuitive abilities more and more. I began to receive information in many different ways from what I refer to as Spirit. All the information was very consistent in that the theme was all about being and sharing how to make choices that allowed for unconditional love to be brought forth through conscious choice here on Earth. As a result, I have created the book, the website, and the Non-Profit organization, as well as a constant and committed effort to share as I live by example. I wouldn't say it has been an easy road, but it has certainly been a fulfilling journey that I am still learning from. Although we are all seemingly different and unique, we all have the same opportunities to choose how to interact with our life experiences. Everyone is really dealing with all the same stuff, just in different degrees and levels of intensity. No matter what the choice to interact lovingly and intelligently is always there for the making!

Every section of this book is going to incorporate some if not all of the other sections. This is because it's all one concept/construct that has many different aspects that all work together. This section is focused on making a conscious choice to co-create a personal shift in your life. It doesn't matter if you have experienced Spiritual awareness before, if you are in tune with your intuition, if you're religious, if you're black, white, red or yellow, or male or female. What does matter is that you're willing to take responsibility for your life and do it in an unconditionally loving way! Everyone can choose to make a change in the way that they view the world as well as their life experiences within it!

So, step number one is to choose to make a change by taking responsibility for your life. Know that your life is happening for you and by you, and begin to make choices that allow for change to occur where necessary. Understand that interaction and communication through your thoughts, words, behaviors, feelings, and actions with others are reflective of your relationship with yourself. How you choose to communicate can be a beautiful gift to all that is. As we choose to honor and respect ourselves and others we honor our population as a whole. Choose to make a shift and take full responsibility for your life.

Channeling Through Susan: *We are here and excited to share that as you allow for beauty into your life in the form of unconditional Love, a transformation occurs. It is of the utmost importance for as many as possible to choose empowerment through unconditional Love for themselves with in their relationships. It is time for the separateness to end and a united front to unfold. Of course we would love for all to request the guidance and wisdom that is able to enter through their Higher Selves and to begin to implement those choices that allow for peaceful interaction to occur. It is our desire for your relationships to be founded in principles that allow for honor, respect, empowerment through unconditional love, responsibility, and honesty. All of these things facilitate a more joyous and peaceful environment for all to cohabitate in. Use your moments for choices that uphold these principle and be easy on yourself as you make these changes. Because of course it is not about putting pressure on yourself, rather it is about your ability to love and honor yourself and your fellow spirits in human form as you expand together. We love you so much*

Taking the High Road

This expression is a perfect way to remember how to interact with your life experiences. There is more meaning here than meets the eye. Similar to Living in the Light, Taking the High Road means to choose those things which honor and respect yourself and others. What a wonderful way to live. In choosing the "High" road and the thoughts, words, behaviors, feelings, and actions that go with it you are connecting to your Higher Self. We all have a Higher Self; that part of us that knows what the most appropriate and empowered thing to do is. Our Higher Self does not exist outside of truth and responsibility, because it is directly connected to the source of infinite wisdom that we all have access to all of the time. We access it through our choices as we live our lives as Human beings upon Mother Earth. In other words if you are choosing to participate in jealousy, resentment, greed, hate, lies, etc. you are not dealing with your Higher Self because that is not what the Higher Self is.

Again, everything is connected and is an indicator for you to monitor yourself. Pay attention to your own ways of interacting and see where you are. Of course as we go through this process we are going to uncover all sorts of areas that we are able to change. After all, it's a waking up process in the many different areas of your life. Take it step by step and little by little and be easy on yourself, but not too easy on yourself. Your self motivation will be very important in your ability to make changes that require you to step outside of the box you've been living in. Remember, once you step outside one box, you will be living in a different place that you will get to step out of as well! Always be open to this process and enjoy each place that you find yourself in. It is a limitless way to live that allows for the principles of the construct to be applied no matter where you are in your presence and awareness!

As you make these changes, be open to communicating with Divine wisdom. By this I mean wisdom from the Angelic Realm, your Spirit Guides, the Ascended Masters, and so on. The more you choose to "Take the High Road" the closer in vibration you become with this wisdom. You are literally clearing a path way for the "higher" vibration to enter! You're tuning your channel to their station! It is also very important to request this guidance to come into your life. The wisdom and guidance that is always around us is ours to receive, but we must ask for it. We must use our free will choice to request the wisdom and then use our free will choice to become what we have learned, integrating and implementing the wisdom into our lives.

In order to make these changes, you have to remain committed to your choice to lead your life in a different way by "Taking the High Road." It's easy to identify those things that aren't the "High Road." Each individual expresses themselves through their thoughts, words, behaviors, feelings and actions. This is where the work is. You must become an observer of your ways of expressing yourself. What thoughts do you have, what words do you use, what behaviors do you exhibit, what feelings do you feel, and what actions do you take. Since we know that "The High Road", "Spirit", "God" is only truth, unconditional love, respect, honor and peace, anything other than that isn't it. Let's identify right now the difference between the two vibrations, as well as how to bridge the gap between the two!

Spirit is unconditional love, peace, respect, honor and joy. Thoughts that represent this vibration are loving, joyous, understanding and compassionate, as well as respectful in an empowering way! It's very important to require respect and honor for yourself as well as respecting and honoring others. Words that represent this vibration are "I'm happy for you", "I love myself", "you are doing a great job", "how wonderful that you are able to experience prosperity", "you look lovely", "I am proud of you", "will you share with me how you are feeling", "I don't understand fully what you mean but I respect your position", "I can see that is important to you", "that behavior is unacceptable and disrespectful", "I would love to communicate with you about this in a respectful way". Behaviors, feelings and actions, if in alignment with your thoughts and words will be supportive and representative of what you are thinking, feeling and acting. In other words, if you are truly happy for someone, you'll think how nice it is that are enjoying their life, you'll say that you are happy for them, you'll feel happy for them, and you might give them a hug or shake their hand.

This is where it can get a bit sticky! We often times say one thing and do another or say one thing and feel another. This is where you are able to be the observer of what you are vibrating and identify where you are out of alignment with your Higher Self. The Higher Self functions from and through the heart and the goal is to unite the heart with the mind. This is how we bring "Spirit" into Human form, thus bringing Heaven upon earth through our conscious free will choice. As we learn to use our free will choice in ways that support unconditional love, respect, and honor we invite consciousness, awareness and peace to exist in our experience. So your work is to know what "Spirit" looks like in Human form and then choose to become that. It has to be your choice to live this way! The desire comes from within and it is that desire that brings you the courage and strength and empowerment to journey along this path. It's truly a path of enlightenment!

In order to identify what is of a "high" vibration, it is helpful to know what isn't of a "high" vibration. Once it's written and you have read it, there is no excuse you can use for doing it. If you use thoughts, words, behaviors, feelings, and actions that are of a denser/lower vibration after you know the difference, you have chosen to do it! The purpose for illuminating the path is so that you can consciously choose to journey along it in a different way. Journey, so that you can acknowledge where you are, being present, identify what needs to be changed and make the changes. This is how we can each choose to bridge the gap between an unconscious journey through our lives to a conscious journey that allows "Spirit" to exist in Human form, bringing heaven upon Earth.

Anything that has to do with jealousy, hate, animosity, envy, lying, cheating, stealing, harming another, disrespectfulness, worry, disease(disease), competition, etc. is vibrating at a much denser/lower vibration than what "Spirit" IS. When individuals wine, complain, blame others for their circumstances, seek revenge, etc. they are choosing to be something other than "Spirit" in Human form. They are literally holding themselves separate through their choices from what they are within, from their origin and source. When individuals speak using negative language, they are asking for more of the negative to come to them. It's always a choice to describe where you are in a more positive way that is reflective of where you are going. Of course you must always start from where you are, however speak it so that you are moving toward where you're going, knowing that where you're going is already there. Words like "it's hard", "I'm trying", "I can't", "I'm stuck", for example are not supportive of where you desire to go. Rather they are perpetuating where you are and where you would rather not be anymore. You can choose to say that everything is in divine and perfect order if you can't think of a more positive way to say it. Your feeling place will eventually come up to speed with what you choose to speak.

Channeling Through Susan: We are here and again honored to be interacting with all those who are reading this wisdom. Of course it is the topic of bringing unconditional Love into the Human form that we are here to speak about. Each of you in your bodies are in the point of power! You are able to use your free will choice to express yourselves in ways that uphold and reflect Divinity. As you come to know and take responsibility for what unconditional Love looks like in the Human form you will make wonderful and great use of the gifts that you have provided yourselves with. These gifts have always been within you to access and use as you lead your lives! Now is the time to become more and more conscious of your choices to be that which you came here to be. It is a time for peace...a time to be the change that you would like to see for the world. Become these changes within your life circumstances through your choice of how you experience your life. As you take responsibility for your thoughts, words, behaviors, feelings and actions with yourself and others you choose to become whole. You choose to embrace and love all that is, both masculine and feminine. Of course you may appear to be female or male, but we assure you that you carry the other within you and see it reflecting outside of you every minute of every day! So dear ones, as you choose to be conscious as you journey through your life, you choose to become whole with all that is. Choose to communicate with yourself and others, as these "others" are a part of you as well!! We take great joy and pleasure as we participate in the expansion that you choose for yourself. We are filled with joy as each and every one of you chooses to open your hearts to the unconditional Love that has always existed within you. We so enjoy the beauty of the shifts in perception that allow you to forgive and embrace yourselves and others through your choice to take responsibility for what you are vibrating. As you choose the "High Road" you empower your spirit in Human form to enjoy the journey that you embarked upon so long ago!! Blessing to each and every one of you as you walk the path of enlightenment! We love for you to request and receive our guidance as you journey and know that all is in Divine and perfect order! Blessings, we love you so much!

Forgiveness: Letting go of Right & Wrong

This is a very important section. I think the most important one of all once you make the choice to live in the Light! Forgiveness and letting go of "right & wrong" are directly connected and allow for so much healing to occur. In order to forgive yourself and others, it is necessary for you to first let go of what you believe to be "right & wrong". I really love to discuss this because it's so illuminating and co-creates an immediate shift in your life experience as you make the shift in your perception. The only thing that you can change of your past, is your perception of it! As you change your perception of your past you become more present in the present moment! :) I just love that concept.

As we look at "right & wrong," we must realize that the only reason that you think something is right is because you agree with it! Likewise the only reason you think something is wrong, is because you disagree with it! Furthermore, this belief system that you're choosing to use is based on your past circumstances and what you experienced within them! So it stands to reason that everyone is going to have their own views based on their past experiences. Looking at it from this perspective, you can clearly see how there can't be one who is more right or wrong than another. Also, continue to keep in mind that every person is where they are supposed to be, and everything is in Divine and perfect order!

Alright, the work here lies in those feelings of judgment that are founded in you thinking that someone is right or wrong based on your past experiences that may be clouding your perception. Here is where you can ask how present am I really in my present moment? This is always the question and what we discussed in the earlier section allows you to have some tools that can provide insight if you choose to use them! Take a look at your thoughts, words, behaviors, feelings and actions and see where they are! Are they in the Light or are they founded in a denser vibration.

Often times we cling to what we believe to be "right & wrong" because it feels like the safe place to be and allows us to avoid our own muck. Try replacing the words right and wrong with the term does it serve my highest good! We are going to talk about this at greater length later, but for now it will allow you to get out of the judgment phase and become more introspective. You also need to remember that you can never know everything that another person is working on in their life more than you ever fully know all that you are working on in your life. If this is the case, you can't possibly know what is "right & wrong". There is also the fact that what is "right & wrong" for this time frame may or may not be "right & wrong for a different time frame, whether it be past or future! As you are able to let go of right and wrong in the way that it was perceived prior to this information, you will also be able to forgive much easier. You see if you feel that someone has done something wrong to you, you are actually holding yourself accountable for allowing it to happen! It's just easier to blame someone else than it is to take responsibility for your own choices.

As you shift your perception of "right & wrong," you are able to shift your perception of past circumstances and the people involved in them that you may be harboring dense vibrations in relationship to! It truly is your vibration to everything and everyone that co-creates what you are vibrating and thus what you are drawing to yourself! Isn't that cool! There are so many gifts in being able to forgive and move forward in your life. In forgiving yourself you are forgiving others and in forgiving others you are forgiving yourself!! There are gifts for everyone as forgiveness occurs!

Forgiveness however, doesn't mean that you enable unacceptable behaviors! It is very important to make choices that require respect, honor, truth, unconditional love and responsibility within any relationship. If you require this for yourself, you are empowering yourself as well as those who you require it from. Enabling isn't of a high vibration. Also when you choose to treat other in this same manner, you are gifting yourself as well as others! Those who aren't choosing this for themselves are where they are for a reason and will be just fine in the place that they choose to be. You can move on from there and continue to live in the Light.

Forgiveness is always founded in the Light and is the only way for you to be clear! I guarantee that you did the best you knew how to do in any given circumstance and time frame, as did everyone who was involved. We all have an innate desire to be happy and that is always the underlying intention. Unfortunately, there are many situations that involve past experiences and the memories of them that motivate individuals to do things that are harmful to others! It is not that we want to allow or enable these things, it is that we want to understand that there is a reason that these individuals are in this place. We can forgive that and require for ourselves something that is of a higher vibration! Eventually as we begin to forgive and move on in an empowered way that allows for the Higher Self to come through in our choices, we will co-create a loving peaceful world to live in!

Channeling through Susan: We are excited to interact with you pertaining to thus topic! This topic is of course one that requires great commitment and courage to address, as well as a topic that has great rewards when mastered. There are many of spirits in human form who are still what we would like to call spinning in the dense world of judgment, blame and criticism. We implore each of you to learn to love yourselves and as you love yourselves you will love others. You see dear ones, there is only benefit from forgiveness and resolution of past "traumas" that you may still be carrying with you! As you come into wholeness with the wisdom that you are all of one vibration, one energy, there can be nothing to separate you any longer. It is a time of awakening and growth that allows for Divinity to be present within the Physicality of Earth through the choices that you consciously choose to make while existing as Spirits in Human form. Joy lies within the wisdom that all are of one Divine Plan and now is the time to bring Spirit in to physical form. This is what allows for the collective consciousness to exist and continue to evolve. It is your choice to BE that which you came here to BE that allows for more and more to awaken! As you are able to let go of the judgments that you hold of others you are actually letting go of judgments that you are holding of yourself. It is of course your projections of your own self worth that you throw out onto the world. It is time to take responsibility for these thoughts, words, behaviors, feelings, & actions and move forward in a different way. Your Ancestors have paved a perfect path for you to move forward on, one that allows for the evolutionary process to continue and for peace and joy to emerge through the level of consciousness that is eminent for Mother Earth and all Spirits in Human form at this time! We Love you so much and greatly enjoy being a part of this process with you! We are grateful for the gifts that you are bestowing upon us through your conscious

Does This Serve My Highest Good

This question is one that allows for consciousness to be present in your present moment. It provides a path out of the "right and wrong" place because it is truly of a higher vibration. Your highest good, first of all is relative to where you! Just like everything else you must always start from where you are. Where you are is going to change depending on what you choose and thus your truth, as well as what serves your highest good is going to change, relative to the present moment! You will hear this message repeated over and over again so that it integrates through the repetition of it! This is the evolutionary process, the choice for people to make changes through their conscious choice! These changes are a direct result of their ability to shift their perception of a past circumstance and then implement the changes that are in alignment with the higher vibrational perception! Once you shift you're perception and reconnect with a higher vibrational view point, your truth changes/evolves!

Each section of the book is saying the same thing in from a different standpoint! There are many parts to the same puzzle, but it is all one puzzle and is not complete without one of the pieces! The simplistic concept of it is to become more present in your present moment through your choice to perceive life circumstances from a higher vibrational perspective! Thus, consciously Living in the Light! It is the ability to pay attention to your thoughts, words, feelings, behaviors, and actions that allow for this to happen. They are the clues that you're providing yourself to discern where you really are on your path and if where you are serves your highest good and thus the highest good of all! It is also important to mention here that your highest good does not include enabling yourself or another. Rather it is about discernment of responsibility, truth, honor and respect in that moment with that circumstance. The simplest example to give is that of the alcoholic. The alcoholic has a false sense of happiness when they are drinking but that is not what serves their highest good. Likewise the partner or friends of an alcoholic may be avoiding setting boundaries for the alcoholic because it doesn't make them happy or feel "good" to do so. They are avoiding the one thing that truly would serve the highest good of all. Dis-allowing situations like this provide an opportunity for responsibility, truth, respect, honor and unconditional love to "BE," through requiring for the highest good to be chosen.

Of course in looking at this example, it becomes very apparent that in order to change and evolve, we are absolutely going to experience some of the denser feelings of the physical world that we live in. It is the choice to allow the feelings to exist, accept that this is where you are in this moment and bring unconditional love to it through your conscious choice to choose what serves the highest good of self and thus others and all that is! You see by choosing what serves your highest good you are choosing to reconnect with your Higher Self as well as the collective Higher Self that we are all a part of! As each person does their part we are collectively changing the world through our choice to become more conscious! It's easy to see then, that as we become more conscious of our thoughts, words, behaviors, feelings and actions we are literally raising the collective consciousness of the world that we live in!

Channeling Through Susan: *We are here and of course again very excited to be interacting in this way! There are so many ways that this wisdom comes through to each and every one of you who are awakening at this time! We assure you that everyone is being affected by the choices of others and this is why we share with so many all of the time! The beauty of this universal teaching is such that it shows clearly how you are all one, regardless of the fact that you appear separate or individual as you exist in your physical forms. The wisdom of what we bring forward for you to work with is founded in the knowledge that in fact you are all one, we are all one! It is in this beauty that everything you are experiencing exists. It is also in this beauty that a point of power for each and every one of you exists. As you are able to become more aware of the gift that you each possess, that is to use your free will choice to bring consciousness into physical form through thoughts, words, behaviors, feelings and actions, each and every one of you will become a conscious participant in the evolutionary process! As you learn to discover more about yourself and all that is around and about you, the choice for unconditional love and that which serves your highest good and the highest good of all will be the only choice that you desire! We love you so much and we are here for you always. We are grateful for the opportunity to share this wisdom with you and be part of the growth that is occurring in this most beautiful time frame! Blessings and joy to all*

The Commitment of 100% Responsibility

In a timeframe when we are experiencing many changes, taking 100% responsibility can be challenging sometimes! We look at the world and its state of affairs and wonder what will become of it all! The fact that seems to be so much turmoil occurring right now is an even more compelling reason to begin to integrate and implement this wisdom! In order for change to occur, there must be the opportunity to change. There are so many people who get "comfortable" in their old ways of doing things so that they draw to them circumstances that will allow for change to occur. In other words, the higher wisdom of the Higher Self desires to come forth and be present and there for provides opportunity for change to occur through conscious choice. The opportunity to take responsibility for all that is in our world through the way we interact with it! This is what is meant by taking 100% responsibility!

Of course, again we must always remember that 100% responsibility is relative to the present moment and what we have experienced and come to know up to that point in time. Therefore as always, 100% responsibility is subjective and will continue to evolve as we evolve. That being said, we can also understand that it is through the conscious choice to take 100% responsibility of how we interact and communicate with life circumstances and relationships that allows for everything within and without to change and evolve.

You can only be responsible for how you choose to interact; you cannot be responsible for another's choices. This is an important key to understanding responsibility! You must also remember that in any given circumstance everyone is thinking, speaking, behaving, feeling and acting from a place that is based on what they know to be true in that moment. Furthermore what they know to be true in that moment is based on their feeling place and memories of their past life experiences, in this life time and prior lifetimes! This makes it even more important for everyone to take responsibility for how they interact because every interaction allows for the growth of everyone involved.

I would also like to say at this point that I realize this information can be a bit overwhelming and serious to look at. The purpose of it really is to allow for more peace and joy to flow! As we learn to choose to be easier on ourselves in the way that we perceive things and bring more laughter and a sense of humor into our lives, we also co-create and evolve. That is not to say one should allow or enable those things that are disrespectful, we just own and take responsibility for how we relate to them. Everyone is only responsible for themselves through their choices and of course we are also responsible for our choices to be responsible for those relationships that require union and team work.

What I am referring to here are those relationships, like intimate partners, children, parents, coworkers, etc. Just like anything, every circumstance has its own dynamic! Those situations that involve other human interaction are the most important for growth. This is so because you are literally interacting with parts of yourself "outside" of yourself. As you are able to desire what serves your highest good as well as what serves another's highest good that you are involved with, unconditional love is able to enter the Earthly vibration in a beautiful way! Through caring for your spouse, your children, your friends, etc. you are able to choose to give and receive! You are able to choose and require respect and honor as well as truth and responsibility in so many ways that wouldn't be possible without someone to share the experience with! It is important to go within, but it is just as important to go to the "outside world" as well!! Why? Because remember, what is within is without and what is without is within. If we really live by the knowledge that we are all one, then we know that all those who are in our circumstance are one with us and we are one with them. Therefore, how we interact with everyone is a reflection of how we feel about ourselves as well as others!

So as we choose consciously to take 100% responsibility, remember that we are all one! We appear as though we're separate as we move about the Earth, but we truly are all part of one beautiful vibration. Choose to look at things from this perspective, knowing that what we choose to think, speak, behave, feel and act have a direct affect on all that is through our unique, individual and beautiful physical form. Let's use our point of power for a Divine purpose that allows for the unconditional love of our source to be brought into physical form! I know we can all do it!

Channeling through Susan: As we are here to speak with you, we would like to express our joy and gratitude for this process and our part within it! We are so excited for each and every one of you to experience this wisdom for yourselves. For as you begin to choose differently for yourselves, you are choosing differently for all that is. This is your gift to the whole that is able to emanate and radiate to you and through you as you lead your lives as spirits in human form. Your ability to take responsibility for your choices, is of course of the utmost importance. We would impress upon each of you to know that you are love and that it is your point of power to choose consciously to "BE" the unconditional love that you originate from through your choice to interact in that way. Know and remember that all is in Divine and perfect order and choose from this place of higher vibration to live! We love you so much and we thank you for your gifts!

The Commitment of 100% Truth

100% Truth sounds a bit daunting, but it is so important. Our truth is of course relative to the present moment as well, and our ability to address it is so important. 100% truth goes hand in hand with 100% responsibility. You must have one to have the other! They are a union and when you commit to choosing the union of 100% responsibility and truth you are choosing also to open your heart and connect to the higher self and the beautiful energy of our source! Living in the Light is opening your heart! One Love, One Light, One Heart…we are all one.

So speak your truth, discover what makes your heart sing. As you speak the truth to yourself and others do it with compassion, empowerment, respect, and love for not only yourself but those who you are interacting with! When you choose to fib or lie, you are lying to yourself more than the other person. What you are communicating to yourself is that you aren't deserving of the beauty that is here for you. Really, the person that suffers the most when you choose to lie is yourself! As you are suffering, you are consciously choosing to have others suffer too! Remember we are all one. When you choose to avoid confrontation with a circumstance or a significant person in our life, you are creating a weak foundation that is based on out-of-integrity behaviors.

Truth allows for trust to occur as a foundational part of any relationship. It is so important to know and trust that those around you are telling the truth! Lying is manipulation which is certainly not founded in the light! The purpose for all of the information in this work book is to bring everything out on the table! If you clearly know the difference between Living in the Light and the denser vibrations, there can be no excuses anymore for your thoughts, words, behaviors, feelings and actions! The wisdom provides an opportunity to function in a more clear way in your second by second daily lives through conscious choices made, based upon this wisdom. It also allows for Divinity to flow more freely and more frequently.

So, be honest with where you are so that you can move forward in a different way that serves your highest good and the highest good of all that is. Be easy on yourself, but at the same time be committed to doing the work and choosing consciously to be 100%responsible and truthful from where you are, so that you may experience new truths through your awareness.

Channeling through Susan: As we speak about the importance of truth we must also speak about the ancestors that have brought forth with every generation their truths! You see dear ones, as with every generation of the past, you are all provided a platform upon which to stand that provides an opportunity for evolution to occur. This is part of the process of awakening and becoming conscious of what you are choosing to "BE." Here is where the empowerment lies. You can choose to exist in a world of blame, self doubt, jealousy and judgment, or you can choose to tell yourself the truth! The truth is that where you are in the present moment was brought forward to you by the ancestral love line that has preceded every single one of you and your families. You are who and what you are because of the truths and choices that have been made and laid before you in this time frame! This is why we love so much to tell you that you are in the point of power! You are now standing on a platform of the past and have the opportunity to choose consciously in the present moment and carry the whole forward in a higher vibrational way! Oh we love so much to see the looks in your eyes when you realize that all is well and that all is in Divine and perfect order! As you tell the truth, you must forgive, and as you forgive you are taking responsibility for what you are choosing! Now dear ones you are getting it, now you are becoming more conscious as you dwell in your physical bodies and thus becoming the Spirits in Human form that you have incarnated to be! Find a way to love all that has brought you to this point of power in your existence! Be grateful for the opportunity to choose consciously how you are going to move forward from that point into the future. Of course the only thing that you can change of the past is your perceptions of it. It is this shift in perception that allows for Light to enter and unconditional to be present now and as you move forward into the future! We Love you so Much!

The Commitment of 100% Forgiveness

Like 100% responsibility and truth, 100% forgiveness requires the other two! They are a trinity that allow for evolution to occur. Our world is fixated on war, right and wrong, judgment and blame and jealousy and greed. All of these are founded in the denser vibrations and can be used in a beautiful and positive way! Yep, they really can! If we can remember that everything is in Divine and perfect order and that it is always how we interact with something rather that reacting to it, we can begin the process of change in a positive higher vibrational way! When we understand that everyone has a basic desire to feel happy we can immediately remember that everyone is functioning from where they are in that moment based on their past experiences. Maybe they haven't learned yet that they are able to make a difference through becoming a more conscious and responsible human being!

When you can hold onto this knowing, you are providing pathways for forgiveness to open. This doesn't mean to enable the behavior, it just means not to participate in the behavior from a denser view! You see if you participate in the denser behavior by choosing thoughts, words, behaviors, feelings and action that are dense, you are no different than the other individual. You are simply the other side, the reactive side of that behavior! If however, you can stop, look, listen and INTERACT, you will begin to see and hear something very different! Oh, I can hear all of you right now thinking to yourself, "that's a lot easier said than done." I get it, and I will have to agree with you, it's not always the easiest thing to do! It is however a very rewarding thing to choose!

My personal experience has been that the more you make the choice to perceive things in this way, the easier it gets!! Spirit loves to remind people in sessions/readings not to use the words that it's hard, I can't, I'm trying, etc.! The purpose it to remind us that our words are reflective of our thoughts, our thoughts are reflective of our feelings and our feelings are reflective of our past! The degree that our past is still programmed and running in our present moment is the degree to which we are present in our present moment! So, when you begin to understand that our thoughts, words, behaviors feelings and actions are all literally connected, you can clearly see the importance of paying attention to the words we use.

To tie this all together here, if we are using words that represent judgment, blame, jealousy, anger, etc. that means we are holding onto feelings that are attached to our past circumstances. We then hold others accountable outside of us through reactive behaviors that are founded in the projection of our own low self esteem. We really just want to feel better about ourselves, because we feel that we should have been able to do something to stop what occurred, we really are still blaming ourselves. So you see, when we can forgive another and understand that they were doing their best with what they know or knew, we are also forgiving ourselves for not doing something wrong! This choice allows us to move forward in a new way making different choices that allow for the higher vibrations to enter into our physical experience! Also, when we forgive ourselves for things in our past and acknowledge that we were doing the best with what we knew at the time, we begin the process of forgiving those who were involved. This is what allows for interaction with the higher vibrations and co-creates new pathways that no longer exist in the denser vibrations!

Forgiving yourself and others sets all involved free of the past circumstance and allows for peace to enter in new ways! Our lives here can be filled with joy in everyday no matter what is in your experience! There truly is a gift in everything! If you haven't recognized the gift in a circumstance yet, then find the gift in something else that is easier to see. Because, where your attention goes your energy flows and when you choose for yourself to pay attention to something more positive and beautiful, you're also choosing to bring more clarity into your vibration. As you choose for more clarity to come in, it allows for you to think more clearly about those things that aren't so clear yet! This is Living in the Light! Choose to take responsibility of how you interact and communicate, tell yourself the truth, and forgive so that everyone can move forward in a more healthy way!

Channeling through Susan: As we speak about forgiveness we are speaking about the embodiment of unconditional Love! It is one of our favorite topics. This is so because it is what we are and also what you are. As you wake up and reconnect to the beauty that lies within you, clear pathways that allow for more and more divinity to flow to you and through you! We are always your cheerleaders and your support system as you journey through this process. Of course we have compassion for you as choose this journey, because it involves you having to interact with many things that you have been hiding from for some time! We know this is a bit challenging at times, but oh it is a wondrous process! If you can just redefine a bit for yourself, the meaning of what you are experiencing, it will ease the process for you somewhat! We are going to liken it to the healing of an injury that you sometimes experience in you human forms. In other words, there is physical pain as you perceive it through the healing process, and then it is gone because it has healed. Also we love the example of your babies when they are born. Each of you is excited for the baby despite the fact that you experience physical symptoms through the birth process, as well as many times through their growth process!:) It is a gratifying experience in many ways that allows for growth to occur with all involved. The evolutionary process is very similar to what we are sharing here! Keep up the wonderful work that each of you are choosing! When you choose for one you choose for all! We love you so much!

The Commitment of Observation

Observation is a tool that allows us to clearly look at what we are thinking, speaking, behaving, feeling and acting! This is such an important part of taking 100% responsibility of our lives and the circumstances we are interacting with! First you choose to take responsibility for your life circumstances and the way that you interact with them through your communication. Also of great importance is to be sure that you choosing this because you desire to. In other words, be sure you are not choosing it because someone is telling you to. The whole purpose of this wisdom is that individual's make the shift from it's happening to me, to it's happening for me and by me. Therefore, it's clear why it must be your choice to desire to take responsibility for how you interact and communicate with yourself and others.

Observation is the tool that allows you to discern if where you are is serving your highest good and the highest good of others. This is an important discussion for relationships of any kind as well! Of course, you always have to look first if what is occurring serves your highest good. Then, you have to look at the relationships in your life that you have chosen to be a part of. There is a responsibility there as well! What have you chosen to be? A husband, a wife, a parent, a best friend, a daughter or son, and employee, a doctor, a garbage man, a cashier, a lawyer, etc. Whatever roles you are playing must be a part of the equation as well! It goes back to the old saying of "Be the best that you can be."

Knowing what you know about Spirit/vibration/Source, you realize now that we are all one. You know that what is within is reflected outside of us and what is outside of us is within. This is why it is so important to interact in an unconditionally loving way from within, as well as within all our surroundings. When you realize that you are interacting with yourself even when you are interacting with your husband, wife, children, etc. it gives you a different perspective to work with. The goal is to have everyone working together, knowing that we are all one. Knowing that we are all unique and different aspects of the same whole, sheds light on the importance of Living in the Light! The desire to work together, from our unique perspectives, automatically co-creates a shift into honoring and respecting each other. Integrating and implementing the knowledge of what denser and higher vibrations look like, sound like, and feel like in physical form, allows for observation and choice to occur. Here is the work:

- Request the guidance of spirit

- Always pay attention to your intuition and the synchronicities that are occurring in relationship to any circumstance.

- Always remember there is a positive intention behind every action

- Remember everyone is where they are supposed to be

- Observe what's in the moment

- Accept what's in the moment with gratitude

- Discern whether or not it serves your highest good and the highest good of those you are in relationship with

- Choose consciously your thoughts, words, behaviors, feelings, and actions that move you toward a higher vibrational place, using truth, honor, and respect as your guide

- Communicate clearly with yourself and others, being honest, empowered and compassionate

- Remember that we are all one!

This is Living in the Light! These tools and techniques can be applied to every circumstance and relationship in your life. As you choose consciously to live in this way you are choosing to "BE" the change that you desire to see in the world. We are all here living our lives, some of us consciously and some of us unconsciously, yet others of us are somewhere in between. If we can each choose to have a common goal that will allow for a higher level of consciousness to enter into physical form, we can become a more peaceful, loving, caring and truthful society. I believe that we all have it within us and we're helping each other wake up! Why not shift our perceptions to a more positive and unconditionally loving view? Let's make every choice count! I know we can do it.

Channeling Through Susan: We are here and excited to share on this topic! Of course we revel in your abilities to wake up from your slumber and choose to be the observer in your own life circumstances. It is through these observations that you are able to participate consciously in your own evolutionary processes. As you begin to allow the loving energies of your source through, we are able to communicate with you easier and more clearly. It is our desire for each and every one of you to know the love that is here for you now and that in fact has always been there. It is only through the observations of a denser field that you have held yourself separate from that which we are always offering. You see dear ones, when you are busy judging others for what they choose you are ultimately judging yourselves. We are not of a judgmental vibration, therefore you are not able to feel the joy and love that we are and that you are when you are choosing other than it! We understand that there are many of you who understand this conceptually, but we would like to share that it is now the time to BE the Unconditional love that you inherently are! As you are able to observe yourselves as the beautiful Spirits in human form that you are, choosing to Be the Higher vibrations will allow you to come to a better feeling place within and without! Be courageous as you journey, be committed as you journey, most of all dear ones, be loving as you journey! We love you so much and are pleased to be on this journey with you!

What is Unconditional Love

Unconditional love is many things! It may be things that you wouldn't expect it to be! Some of the main criterion for unconditional love are honoring, respecting, truthfulness, and forgiveness. It is in the ability to be these things to others, as well as to require them by others for yourself. If you are to love others, you must love yourself and if you are to love yourself you must love others. So as we choose to require for those who we interact with to treat us with respect, honor who we are, and have truthful communication with us we then are experiencing unconditional Love. When I say requiring, I don't mean making them or telling them they have to do it. I mean that if someone chooses to treat you in a disrespectful way, it is your responsibility to stop it from happening again. In other words, we have to stop enabling disrespectful behavior that's in our life.

Enabling is actually disrespectful to both parties involved, the one dishing it out, as well as the one receiving it. The one receiving it is disrespecting themselves by allowing it and disrespecting the other by not providing an opportunity for the person stop. Disrespectful behaviors will continue as long as they are allowed to continue. There is no difference in vibration of the enabler or the enable. They are both different parts of the same vibration. Unconditional love includes the empowerment of requiring others to respect you and thus you respecting yourself. Choose to be around those who are respectful and interact with those who are not only if and when necessary. You will notice that

I said interact!! It's our reaction that often indicates we need to make a change, one that will allow for a more positive unconditionally loving response.

We only have control and can take responsibility of what we choose and how we choose it. We never have control or can take responsibility for another's choices. This is such an important point to remember. It's really so much like the 2 year old that tests his or her boundaries and will do what he or she knows they can get away with. It's much less attractive in adults. This is an important part of unconditional love and one that we have challenges with. It's easy to love those who love us and it's easy to forgive those who we can understand. It seems to be much more challenging to stand up to those who we intimidated by while loving them at the same time. Or to forgive the one who has seemingly done a terrible thing that has somehow altered our life in what we perceive to be an undesirable way!

If we can remember that although we may not agree with or understand what another has chosen we can know that they have a reason for choosing it. At this point we can choose consciously from the present moment how to interact with it. This is where clarity is able to be present, when we are observing, interacting and communicating in an unconditionally loving way! These choices will allow peace to flow more freely between us in our relationships.

The easier part of unconditional love is obvious. "Love they neighbor as thy self," comes to mind here. "Do unto others as you would have others do unto you." These Golden Rules explain unconditional love as well as anything can! If we can slow down our daily lives just a bit and pay attention to what is going on around us, we can choose to interact in loving ways with everyone and everything we encounter. Pay it forward, smile at others, share with others, help others, be kind to animals, be loving to Mother Earth, be kind and loving to yourself. It's really pretty simple when you get down to it. Just choose it!

Channeling Through Susan: We oh so love this topic…it is our very favorite. There is more joy and peace here for each and every one of you than you can imagine! Unconditional Love is what we are and what you are as well! It is the empowerment of it that allows for more of it to flow to you and through you out into the world. In other words dear ones, we always honor your choices whether you choose to go toward the denser vibrations or closer to the higher vibrations of the spiritual realm. We don't love you any less for what you choose, we are always here waiting for your return to that which you inherently are. So as you in your human forms choose more and more to be unconditional love, the more unconditional love you will experience. Joy will become more visible as you perceive your life circumstances from a different vantage point, one that is outside of judgment, founded rather in acceptance and forgiveness. We do not recommend that you accept everything into your experience in the sense that you should expose yourself to it, rather that you accept what is in your life circumstance in every moment and choose how to interact with it! You see dear ones; this is your work in this time frame. It is this work that allows for the evolutionary process to occur! We cannot express enough the love that is here for you that already exists within you. It is our desire for you to reconnect, re-member that which you are and that which you have come to bring into consciousness through the human form, into the physical world. This is the gift that you are able to share with yourself and all that is. You are able to know and understand that even as the masculine and the feminine seem to be different and separate, they are one. You who appear to be women carry the man with in, and you appear to be men carry the women with in! This is your gift as well! As you are able to integrate this knowing and begin to interact with yourself outside of yourself, you will begin to awaken. There isn't one among you who isn't part of the whole that you live in! Are you beginning to see the "Light"…we know that you are. It is our purpose to share as many times and in as many ways as possible with all who will listen, and hopefully hear, that your world can be different than what you see as you shift your perceptions of what you know to be true! We are blessed and honored for this time with you and are very grateful for your work. Blessings

Finding Peace in the Pain

I think that finding peace in the pain is our biggest challenge. It is what we are all learning about right now. How many times have we heard the phrase "where your attention goes, your energy flows," and of course we all know that where our energy flows is what we get more of! Ugh!!! So how do we become accomplished at feeling better when we feel like crap? There are of course all sorts of wonderful books already written about all of this, I personally think the more the better! It's time we figure it out together so that we can move forward in a different way, a more peaceful loving way. Speaking for myself, this has been my greatest challenge and I'm still working on it!

I think the key lies in our ability to redefine the goal. What I mean is, I think many of us think we shouldn't be angry or sad or jealous or any of the feelings that fall in that category. The truth is that if that's what you're feeling than you had better acknowledge that you're feeling that way. If you deny it, you're lying to yourself and others. The trick is not to stay there! You don't want to flounder in the muck, you want to swim or wade through it to a higher vibration than where you are. It's different for everyone because we all have our own experiences that present themselves through our feeling which are representative of our memories.

The wisdom here is the same as knowing what is true for you now may not be true for you later. You see as we evolve, we shift our perceptions which change our truth the same way as we can learn to feel peace within a painful process. There is always a way to feel better about something, the key is in your choice to do it. When you're feeling sad, your next better feeling is less sad but still not joyous. As we learn to release the expectation of holding ourselves to standards that limit us, we are able to allow the feelings to emerge for what they are rather than what we think they should be. Its sounds like it would be really easy to just be present in the moment and allow what is to be. The thing is, what is, is different for all of us because we all have different perspectives and memories that are related to what is occurring. We have to learn to heal from the inside out. Fortunately it is often from the outside in that we get the opportunity.

As we lead our lives, what we have experienced in the past continues to vibrate with us until we change it. We see it outside of us in our life circumstances, specifically in our relationships. In order to heal from within, we draw to us those life circumstances and relationships that provide us opportunities to interact with what we think, speak, behave, feel, and act. It's really quite a beautiful thing. This is why the saying the world is a reflection is really true. It may not always be an exact reflection of whom or what we are, but it is a perfect reflection of something that we need to work on through our choice to interact with rather than react to.

Again, it's always a bit more challenging to be at peace with pain than it is to be at peace with peace. We can do it. We all have the tools and the courage to "Live in the Light" regardless of how much darkness we perceive. Of course, as usual, it is always our choice that allows for this to come into being. It takes courage and commitment to walk this path.

Channeling through Susan: We are here and it is our pleasure to interact with you pertaining to this topic! This is a subject that is of the utmost importance for us to address with you, for it is the "State of Affairs" so to speak. What we mean by this is that it is a time of great importance and one that allows for much healing to occur if you will choose to do it! Of course in your human world of physicality, the emotional status of you're being is directly related to your physical health, as well as your psychological health. It is our intention to share with you, wisdom that will assist you in moving forward along your path in a more peaceful way. This, we know, can be a bit of a challenge for you sometimes. We assure you that you are quite capable of journeying through the emotional "discomforts" and consciously choosing to bring yourself to a better feeling place. It is this process and your ability to navigate through it that will allow for transformational healing and evolution to occur. As you are able to accept the feeling of pain that may surface in your circumstances, you will have taken the first step in bringing in a different perception. These dear ones will provide an opportunity for you to move toward forgiveness of yourself and others. There is a peaceful way to coexist within every feeling you may encounter and we would like to remind you that you are drawing those circumstances to you through your vibration. You are living breathing beacons for those circumstances that will provide you opportunities to move forward on your path, through your choice to interact with responsibility, honesty, and unconditional love. Pain is relative to what you have experienced as well; redefine that which you perceive to be painful dear ones and you will find peace in any situation that you choose to. Be easy on yourselves as you journey, for you are sacred, beautiful, light filled beings living as "spirits in human form!" we love you so much and are always a part of everything you do!

Communication or Confrontation

Communication is the key to any relationship. By the way, you have a relationship with everything in your life, how you communicate with it or about it, with yourself and others determines your vibration pertaining to it. Communication involves responsibility, honesty and respect for yourself and others. Be open to the idea that you are the only one responsible for how you feel and at the same time are respectfully caring and attentive to those who you are in relationship with and their feelings. Choose for it to be important to you, how your loved ones feel and remember that your actions have an impact on all of your relationships. So, although you are not responsible for someone's feelings, you are responsible for how you communicate and interact with each relationship.

Communication occurs in many ways, both consciously and unconsciously, as well as a mix of the two! We speak loudly, often times without ever opening our mouths! You communicate with your eyes, your actions, your behaviors and mannerisms, and often times through your silence! We also communicate sometimes in a manner that involves a conscious choice that is clouded by unconscious denser feelings. This type of communication is very self serving and destructive. Everyone functions from a desire to feel good, including the people who make choices that are self-serving at another person's expense. This is where your work lies; these are the behaviors that it is time to change. If we can become aware and pay attention to how we interact and communicate with our loved ones and others around us, we can choose to be a more loving individual that creates strong communicative relationships in our lives!

Conscious/unconscious communication occurs when you make a choice to intentionally do or say something but are not thinking about how it may affect others. In other words, when you're so caught up in your own feelings that you think, feel, speak, and choose actions that affect another person adversely, you're consciously choosing actions that are unconsciously affecting others in an adverse way. This is what I mean by conscious communication that is founded in unconsciousness. Once you become aware of the knowledge that you must take responsibility and be truthful in your choices to act, you can choose consciously/intentionally to make loving choices for all, not just yourself. Of course your truth is always shifting as you allow for new perceptions to be chosen. However consciously choosing to withhold information, fib, lie, embellish, or do something that you are aware is hurtful to yourself or others is what I would call a conscious unconscious choice. Better known as avoidance behavior! This is a choice that does not support a strong truthful communicative foundation in any relationship!

Avoiding something that we know should be verbally communicated is in the lying family! The choice to avoid is in essence the choice to lie. Like everything else there are varying degrees of lying, but it is all of the same vibration. Lying is always attached to fear and guilt and the "I'm not good enough" energy. In the end, you're only lying to yourself by choosing not to speak your truth in that moment. On another level, it is a sign that it's time you begin to tell yourself the truth about the loving Spirit in Human form that you are. You see when you choose to fib, your only avoiding your own vibration that desires to evolve. Via law of vibration, we draw to ourselves those circumstances that provide us opportunities to take responsibility and be truthful, loving, empowered Spirits in Human form.

Some circumstances may feel uncomfortable at the time, but it is our ability to identify where we have areas that still need some work and make the changes necessary for spoken communication to occur. Since we know that what is in our outer circumstance is coming from within our inner vibration, we can always remember that it truly is there for a reason…and this reason is to take the opportunity to change old patterns that don't facilitate truth, integrity, and love, rather than using the term "everything happens for a reason" as an excuse to continue these old destructive patterns. It's how we choose to interact and communicate with it that allows for changes to occur or for nothing to change. If we choose to change nothing, we will perpetuate old patterns that may not serve our highest good anymore! If we desire to change, we must first have the circumstances that provide opportunities for change and then consciously choose to be the change that we say we desire within the old pattern.

Honesty truly is the best policy. Treating others as we would like to be treated is an easy and clear way to live, what we do to others we are doing to ourselves and our creator! We have to start by telling ourselves the truth and then communicating with ourselves and in our relationships in a respectful way to everyone! This is a great tool to remember as you begin to be the observer and take action based on your observations. Pay attention to what you and others think, speak, behave, feel and act. Are yours and others thoughts, words, behaviors, feelings and actions in alignment with each other? In other words, are you or they saying one thing and doing another, are they saying they are something but behaving in a way that is inconsistent with it? It's easy to see once you take responsibility for whom and what you choose for yourself. An example of this is someone who describes themselves as a loving person and yet judges others, or someone who says they are honest yet frequently chooses to lie, fib, avoid, withhold, or embellish! This is where the opportunities exist for our individual transformation. Because we know that we are all one, as we choose to shift our perceptions and make changes in our choices we also assist in transforming the world around us!

As you choose to be honest, you automatically choose to require others to be honest. As you choose to communicate, you automatically require others to communicate with you. As you choose to respect yourself, you choose for others to respect you as well! This is what taking responsibility for your life looks like! No more excuses, it's you who chooses to be where you are and it's you who chooses to be what and who you are. Your relationships with those who are the closest to you are the most important. Those that you love are those with whom you spend the largest amount of time with. What type of foundation have you built through your communication? Is it honest, respectful, caring, and unconditionally loving, or do you avoid conversations and interactions?

This is the most important work of all! If you are avoiding conversations and interactions with those you love, you are avoiding yourself and creating a weak foundation that is bound to crumble. In this case, confrontations often occur. By confronting, I mean that there's an energy of combativeness, usually founded in fear, guilt, and insecurity. What a wonderful opportunity to make a change. By observing and taking responsibility for your own feelings, you can make a different choice and change the behavior. That's the only way to co-create a solid foundation for yourself and thus your relationships. How important is your relationship to yourself and others? You will be able to tell by how committed you are to taking responsibility, being truthful, being supportive, and being compassionate, as well as being unconditionally loving. By unconditionally loving I mean choosing not to enable disrespectful unhealthy behaviors from yourself or others! This is how a strong foundation is built. As you desire this for yourself, you choose it for yourself.

This is actually a very important aspect of this work. You must choose it for yourself. It's a red flag if within your relationship you feel like you have to do something because someone is telling you to. This is an egoic behavior that arises from a rebellious place and a dishonest place. This occurs when someone is not communicating with another and it creates separateness within the relationship. If you truly care about yourself and others, you choose to do and know the things that allow for truth to be present rather than behaviors that involve untruths. Living in the Light means choosing to live in an honest, unconditionally loving way with yourself and others; it's the only way to co-create a lasting foundation that will support the relationships in your life. If you have to "confront" something that's uncomfortable for you, choose to communicate your way through it and pay close attention to your thoughts, words, behaviors, feelings and actions as well as those who you're interacting with! Choose to bring each feeling to a better feeling place!

Communication is so closely related to truth and responsibility that I feel it's very important to spend some more time on this topic. The more wisdom that is presented on this subject, the greater the awareness and level of consciousness that will occur. The goal of this book is to present a perspective that will allow individuals to view the way they navigate through their life circumstances from a different perspective. It is truly an awakening process that requires the desire and willingness to be open to change.

I'd like to speak more to the nature of truth. Truth is extremely subjective. Truth is always shifting and is always relative to the circumstance, as well as each individual perception of a circumstance. Of course every individual's perception is founded in their feelings which are representative of their past experiences. You can see how the nature of truth is a tricky thing to interact with. That's why the ability to observe and pay attention to a construct that provides tools founded in universal wisdoms is so important. You are the only one who can know your own truths and how to communicate them. As you communicate them to others through your speaking of them, you set the stage for yourself to come into alignment with who and what you are stating that you are.

Remember that every Spirit in Human form is always functioning on the intention of feeling good. The question then becomes are these intentions serving all involved, or are they only self serving with disregard to those around you. Discernment is of great importance here for yourself and others you are in relationship to. Are the truths that you and others are speaking of consistent with and in alignment with your thoughts, feelings, behaviors and actions in that moment? Are the truths that you are speaking consistent from circumstance to circumstance over the course of time? This is where the work is, this is the evolutionary process at this time. Becoming aware, choosing to be conscious of who and what you are projecting and being; then making changes according to what serves your highest good and path of best destiny!

You may observe circumstances that involve individuals or yourself speaking one truth in one moment and then speaking a different truth on the same subject in another moment. Here is where truth can be seen as subjective. Because our truth is directly related to our feeling place, our truth in any moment can be different depending on our past experiences that we have not yet brought into the light. (Brought into the light, in the sense that we still harbor anger, resentment, hurt, sadness, etc. within our vibration in relationship to a past circumstance that we experienced.) Again this is where the work is. When we can recognize this within ourselves, it's an opportunity to heal. The healing process occurs as we can tell ourselves a new truth about the circumstance so that we can experience it in a different way! Preferably a better feeling way! There are always gifts in every circumstance and it's our choice to discover what those gifts are that allow for our evolutionary process to occur.

Truth is also subjective in the sense that there are many different truths within any given situation. For example, let's say that your mother in-law, whom you don't see very often, gives you a gift that you really don't care for much. The truth is that you don't like it and don't want to keep it. The truth also is that she was excited to give you something that you would like. The truth is that you want to let her know how much you appreciate her thinking of you and taking the time to pick something out for you. Or maybe the truth is that she hasn't taken the time to get to know you and what you like. The point here is that there are always many moving parts to every circumstance and every moving part will touch on the vibrational parts that you have running with in you.

An individual who is in a secure place within themselves might interact with this circumstance by saying thank you so much for thinking of me, I really appreciate the gift. Thus interacting with that aspect of the truth and choosing to honor the person's intentions rather than the gift itself. A person, who has a more insecure energy actively running, might have some anger for the fact that this person doesn't take the time to get to know what they really like and react to the situation. You get the idea! It's your relationship to everything that creates your reality and your perceptions of each circumstance are what create your relationships to everything. Furthermore, your references of what you've experienced are what create your perceptions; and your thoughts, words, feelings, behaviors and actions are fueled by your perceptions and references.

Again, here is the work; shift your perceptions as you choose to observe and change your thoughts, words, feelings, behaviors and actions. As you shift your perceptions, you shift your vibration and thus your point of attraction. As your point of attraction shifts, you begin to draw to you those things that match the new vibration that you are radiating out from within yourself!

So as you observe all that is occurring, choose to interact with the truth that serves the highest good of yourself and others. If you are choosing to withhold solely because you don't want to hurt another's feelings, you may be co-creating a weak foundation. This is especially true for the intimate relationships in your life. I am referring to those relationships in your life that you spend the largest amounts of time interacting with. Your intimate partner, your children, your parents, your best friends, your work family and so on. These relationships require a strong, communicative, supportive, open and honest foundation to be healthy. These are the relationships where you are most able to interact with yourself through those who are "outside" of yourself knowing that we are all one.

Let's co-create a foundation for the world through our choices to be honest and take responsibility for our interactions and communications in our life circumstances and relationships! This is how we can be the change that we want to see in the world. Take responsibility, be honest with yourself and others, be unconditionally loving to yourself and others, and most importantly be open to new perceptions and ideas entering your reality!

Channeling through Susan: We are here and especially excited to speak a bit on this topic! Communication is the key to every relationship. As Spirits in human form, you have free will choice that allows you to co-create your experience here upon Mother Earth. It is our wish for each of you that you use your free will to choose those things that will facilitate a peaceful and loving existence. As each of you embraces the wisdom that you are all one, you will begin to open your hearts in a manner that will allow for unconditional love to enter your experience. It is in this wisdom that lays the opportunity to use your free will choice for truth and responsibility that can only be brought forth in your thoughts, words, behaviors, feelings and actions! Dear ones, this is how you communicate!! Do you see what we are sharing with you? Your thoughts, words, behaviors, feelings, and actions are your communications!!! This is why we say to you that your choice to communicate in an unconditionally loving way is the key! Choose to bring your negative feelings to a higher vibrational place! Choose to communicate through interaction, truth, honor, love, and respect! Do these things and you will be the Spirit in Human form that you have came forth to be. We love you so much and are very much loving the growth that we are witnessing in each of you!

Perception and Opinion

Your perception of something is your ability to choose to observe how you feel and interact rather than react. When you acknowledge that you perceive, you have become aware of the fact that you can shift your perceptions. Perceptions are the stories that you tell yourself about life circumstances that are based on your past experiences. Knowing this allows you to change the stories that you tell yourself so that they are founded in a positive loving vibration. This is where the healing occurs through conscious choice and a feeling journey that leads to forgiveness. This is very different than an opinion.

Your opinions can often be founded in judgment, which is often founded in right and wrong! Right and wrong are based on what you've experienced in the past and how you feel that it affected you. Most often, these feelings that are founded in judgment are unresolved issues that aren't necessarily based on what serves your highest good. Rather they are often founded in denser emotions like resentment and anger and guilt! Take a look at your opinions to see if you're judging, or if you are really expressing what you prefer based on non-judgmental feelings. The goal is always to choose to bring yourself to a loving place. It really is simplistic in concept! Sometimes easier to read about than to do! I know we can do it!

Channeling through Susan: As we discuss this topic, we are happy to share wisdom that will allow for universal and unconditional love to evolve. Of course as you are able to tell yourselves a new story about your current feeling place, you will automatically be shifting the energy of your vibration. What you are vibrating is your gift to the world and the universe! Do you see why we love to share these truths with you in many different ways? The more that you are able to embrace that you are one with the world that you live in, taking responsibility for how you exist in the world becomes your gift to all that is! Monitor your perceptions and opinions dear ones, so that you use your free will to make shifts that allow for higher vibrational energies to enter through your physical forms. This is how we like to share with you that you bring forth Heaven upon Earth! You see Spirit only exists in the loving energies, therefore the more that you choose to "BE" the loving energies, the more you are consciously choosing to interact with Spirit within the Earth plane! Choose to bring Heaven upon Earth through your thoughts, words, behaviors, feelings, and actions! We love you so much and we are with you always!

Acceptance or Avoidance

How "present" are you in the present moment? Acceptance is an important step in the process of healing and the evolutionary process! We must accept where we are as well as where others are in order to be present in the moment. It's important to begin where you so that you can address the feelings that are active concerning the circumstances that exist in your life in any given moment! Presence is truth, responsibility, and respect! Again we are back to these basic and exemplary tools that will continue to be given in a variety of ways. Avoidance behaviors hinder our forward moving progress as individuals and as a whole. When we avoid what is occurring in our experiences we are actually lying to ourselves and others, thus co-creating a weak foundation of relationships in our lives!

As with all of the topics in this work book, each is integrally related to the other! Furthermore, as you have begun to understand they all come back to truth, responsibility, respect and communication! This is the Divine Perspective that I have been receiving and reading about, similar to others, for the last 10 or so years of my life journey. As we learn to accept where we are, where others are, and how we feel about where it all is, we automatically co-create a stronger more solid foundation in which to function from as we live our lives. Acceptance doesn't mean that we have to remain where we are if it is not serving our highest good and path of best destiny! It's actually the exact opposite! When we accept where we are, we are able to discern if what is occurring does serve our highest good and path of best destiny. If it doesn't, we can consciously choose to make a change. Acceptance provides an opportunity for change to occur!

Change is often what we try to avoid! There are many things that will be observed that you'll want to continue being and doing, anything that does serve your highest good and path of best destiny! The point is, acceptance allows for the opportunity for you to be honest and take responsibility for the experiences and circumstances in your life. Acceptance allows for you to make positive changes where they are necessary as well as to make choices to maintain what serves you well! Acceptance also allows you the opportunity to respect and honor where others may be on their journey, even though it may be different from where you are. Although we are all one, each and every one of us has a unique path to walk. Sometimes our paths cross for a time, sometimes we walk together for a very long time, and other times we are on completely different paths. Each path is important in its own unique way and every path and individual provides opportunities for growth in every different circumstance. Sometimes it's an opportunity to stop enabling another and take care of ourself. This is yet another way to respect and support those around us. When you stop enabling destructive behaviors, you provide others with opportunities to grow and choose to become a more honest and truthful person. Choose to accept where you are and interact with it in a forward moving way!

Channeling through Susan: As we share wisdom here we would like to speak about the importance of acceptance and its relationship to truth and responsibility! As each of you in your daily activities are able to accept rather than avoid where you are in relationship to your experiences, you will be consciously choosing to be more of that which you originate from. The ability to accept automatically brings forward truth and responsibility as you interact with what is. Your choice to accept brings forth presence and a level of consciousness that allows for transformation! We love to be a part of your growth through the choices that you make based on the wisdom that you are choosing to integrate into your life! As Spirits in Human form you have light that exists within you. It's through your choice to accept, be honest, take responsibility, choose to co-create change, and the practice of forgiveness, that allows for you to bring that light forth! You see you are all Light beings in Human form and as you each choose to BE, through your actions and communication of truth, love, respect, and honor you become the Light that you already are! This is Living in the Light dear ones, this is the gift that each and every one of you has come here to share. This is why we share what we share with you! It is your birth right to be that which you have come here to be! You must choose it for yourself and then be it through your own accord. It truly is a simple and beautiful gift that you hold with in you, make it your choice to bring it forth through your choices and share it with many. You are all one, treat each other as you would want to be treated yourself! We love you so much...we are one with you!!!

Discernment or Judgment

Discernment is a gift that we can give ourselves and in turn it gifts everyone we interact with! As we learn to let go of judgment, knowing that we are the only ones responsible for our choices and actions, discernment is what allows us to evolve! Judgments are founded in right and wrong rather than what serves our highest good and the highest good of all that is! Remember, right and wrong is founded in our emotional entanglement of past experiences. As we are able to take responsibility for our circumstances as well as our actions, we can discern whether or not our life circumstances are serving our highest good and path of best destiny, making choices accordingly. As we learn to choose through discernment and honesty, we will automatically come into contact with those emotions that require healing. By this I mean forgiving ourselves for the purpose of moving forward in a more healthy way. It is impossible to move forward into the future with clarity if we are clouded by the dense emotions of fear, judgment, anger, resentment or any kind of animosity!

We came here and incarnated into these human bodies with a purpose and a journey to walk. We each have unique and special gifts to share that will allow us to become all that we can be. In this time frame we have come to bring forward a Divine truth and wisdom through our thoughts, words, behaviors, feelings, and actions, that we're all a part of and originated from. It's time to stop judging and blaming ourselves and others and begin to discern and choose those actions that are life affirming, supportive, truthful, respectful, and unconditionally loving to ourselves and others. In order to move forward and evolve, we must have the courage to let go of the denser emotional entanglements that hold us back! The longer we hold onto these dense feelings the longer we perpetuate the same pattern over and over again in our lives! Choose the gift of discernment and free yourself to move forward through your choice to make changes where necessary as well as maintain those things that are working well! Remain in the present moment and be flexible within your life circumstances. Learn to tell yourself a new story, one that is founded in forgiveness and discernment of what serves your highest good and path of best destiny! This is Living in the Light, choosing to be the light through your thoughts words behaviors, feelings, and actions as you exist as a spirit in human form!

What a beautiful way to reunite with what we already are! Our light is always shining within us; it's only by our, or through our, choices to be filled with fear, anger, and judgment, that we remain separate from our unconditionally loving source. As we are able to discern and let go of judgments, we accept love and light into our life! The proof is in the pudding! Meaning; you can say that you are a loving caring person, but your interactions with those in your life will let you know if you truly are what you say you are! When you begin to really pay attention to your choices, you'll notice that there are areas that need work, some more than others! Good for you for making the commitment to take a look at who you really are and how your choices affect your life as well as the lives of others! Choose discernment and make changes that allow for love to flow to you and through you to others. Use honor and respect as your guide as you discern how to move forward through your life. Be the change that you want to see in the world and remember that we are all one! What you do to another you do to yourself and all and what you do to yourself, you do to another and all! Be kind to yourself, you deserve it!

Channeling through Susan: We are excited to speak yet again about the topic at hand, Living in the Light! It is our joy to share with you the importance of this topic in as many ways as we can bring it forth! Here we are speaking of discernment and the importance of letting go of the judgment that so many of you are attached to. You see dear ones, when you feel the need to judge another, you're actually judging yourselves! In some way, shape or form you have forgotten the beauty that lies within you. You are this beauty and it is only by your own hand that you appear to be separate. Separateness is an illusion and can be healed at any time! As you choose to BECOME that which you already are you will journey along the healing path that allows your light to shine. As you shine from within, you will shine on those outside of you as well, warming them with your beauty and presence! These are the gifts that you came to earth to be and share. Choose it dear ones. You're brilliant co-creators here on earth at a time when transformation is occurring. As each of you does their part, the energy of Love, peace and joy will spread across the lands and the bridge between the Heavens and the Earth will form. Each choice you make to be a truthful, loving, respectful, and empowered spirit in Human form will be yet another step that bridges the gap. We love you so much and are honored and privileged at this time to be working with you! Remember we are all one and all that you do affects not only yourself but the whole! Blessings to you all and much love as you journey along your paths!

Interaction or Reaction

Interaction is the goal! It is through interaction within our relationships that we are able to communicate with ourselves and others! Communication means listening to what others are saying as well as being able to express where you are in relationship to what they are saying. As a matter of fact, there is no communication unless both aspects are practiced. Reaction closes down our ability to communicate and thus interaction goes out the window! We react to things that we're afraid of or those past experiences that we have painful memories attached to. So, reaction is a wonderful tool when used as an indicator, a red flag, that there is work to be done.

Use reaction as a sign that you need to heal, release and let go of some emotions that aren't serving your highest good. If you have them, than accept them and begin where you are to tell yourself another story until you can find the peace that exists in every situation. It's always there; sometimes it just takes a bit of work to find it! As you begin this process, you've already stepped into interaction. You're interacting with your own emotions first, which will allow you to interact with those in your life, rather than reacting to them as though they are out to get you! Remember what you have in your experience is always vibrating in some way to your benefit! It's your job to find out how it's to your benefit! Even the most uncomfortable situation can be used to your benefit, and more importantly, as you interact you can discern and choose differently in those areas that require change.

Interaction allows for all of the tools that we have discussed to be integrated into one construct, Living in the Light! It is a Divine perspective and guide to living a peaceful life, both within and without! Remember we are all one. Choose to interact with yourself and others with truth and respect to everyone. Remember that communication is the key to any fundamentally strong relationship. When you choose to be honest and take responsibility, interaction and communication can occur. The lack of truth and responsibility for one's actions, results in reaction and miscommunication that leads to disregard and damage to you and others! Let me be very clear here, you are not communicating or interacting if you are untruthful!! All that can manifest out of that choice is miscommunication and reactive behaviors that are damaging to all concerned! Honesty is truly the best policy! Just Do It! It is what serves the highest good and allows you to BE a more loving and genuine you!

Channeling through Susan: Of course it is our interaction with you at this moment that is a product of your choice to seek and be open to truth and wisdom! It is your choice to interact with us that allows for you to bring a different perspective into your life. As each of you welcomes truth, love, honor, and wisdom into your lives, you're able to affect the whole in a positive way through the individual roles that you play. Through your choices to co-create in this way, alchemization of old patterns that are yearning to be brought forward into the light occurs. The more that you use your free will to choose those things that serve the highest good, the closer you become to that which dwells within you. You see dear ones, it is unconditional love that dwells within you, the beauty of divinity that is the source of all that is! It is through your free will choices to bring unconditional love into the physical world that allows you to interact as a spirit in human form, with heaven upon earth! You see your source is nothing but purity and divinity and love! Therefore, the more you choose to be that which positive pure love is, the closer you are to literally BEING Heaven upon Earth! Is it not beautiful to be the embodiment of what you have come forth in this time frame to be! It is your greatest gift to yourself and all that is that you are a part of! Be the love, be the patients, be the forgiveness, be the kindness, be the respect, be *the honor, be the trust, be the sharing, be the giving, be the change that you desire for your world as you interact with yourself and all that is through your life circumstances! It is your choice what you experience as you journey through your circumstances! Choose to interact in a way that is life sustaining for yourself and those around you! As you choose this for yourself, you will let go of the need to react to circumstances that no longer serve you and ground yourself firmly into being an evolving Spirit in Human form! Each of you have so many wonderful gifts to share with the world, continue to interact with your life in a pure and divine positive way so that you can be your part of the whole to its fullest! Live In The Light through your thoughts, words, behaviors, feelings and actions! Know that we are always with you and ask for our assistance as you journey! We love you so much!*

Was it really meant to be?

There are so many occasions where people say "it was meant to be"! I would like to bring a different perspective to the table here, one that I hope allows for people to think twice about what they choose! We know that we draw to us those things that are a match somehow with what we are vibrating within! We know that our emotional status emanates through our thoughts, words, behaviors, feelings, and actions! We also know that it is ALWAYS our choice as to how we interact with our life circumstances. We know that every life circumstance can be an opportunity to choose positive, high vibrational, life affirming, unconditionally loving choices. We also know that by doing so, we can co create a more truthful, respectful, communicative supportive way of life for ourselves and others! We also know that many frequently choose something different than that! Why?

We are co-creating our future as we spin in the present moment based on what we are holding onto or have healed from our past! Knowing all of what we have just discussed, it follows that our individual choices are an integral functioning piece of the collective whole and that we co-create what unfolds in front of us! So let me ask you, if someone chooses to kill someone, was it meant to be that the other person died? It seems to me that because one person chose to kill another, an outcome occurred that now has to be interacted with! How you interact with any circumstance determines what your outcomes will be! Now the choice is how the family members interact with what happened to their loved one! Will they hold on tightly to anger, revenge, hatred, and blame or will they choose to let go and forgive moving through their pain as best as they can with grace! Both choices have a different outcome, a different "it was meant to be"! In the first case, maybe a family member chooses to take revenge and kill the one who killed their loved one, thus perpetuating the same pattern over again! In the second case, maybe the family member chooses to take actions that bring forth forgiveness without enabling the negative behaviors and work through their pain in a loving and positive way! Of course the second case co-creates a beginning of positive and life affirming interaction that allows for an ending of a pattern of negativity and disregard for life! Which one do you think is meant to be!

We live in a world in which each of our lives is a microcosm of the bigger picture! Each of us is a small part of the whole! Every one of our choices truly has an impact on the whole, as well as on our own individual lives. In the grand scheme of things what I know to be true, is that it's meant to be that we become the loving, peaceful, respectful, life affirming society that we are intended to be! We can co-create this using our free will choices to interact through truthful and unconditionally loving communication with ourselves and others! Every choice provides an outcome that's an opportunity to interact in a life affirming way or a life inhibiting way! What do you want to choose? What do you think should be "meant to be"? Start in your own life and choose to end those life inhibiting patterns, choice by choice, in every circumstance of your life, as you choose life affirming unconditionally loving thoughts, words, behaviors, feelings, and actions! Use every opportunity to begin new life that is filled with positive intention and unconditional love!

This means that we will have to do some challenging work when an uncomfortable circumstance arises for us to interact with! Choose to stop the old patterns that no longer serve us by Living in the Light through your choices. I know we can do it! All of us have what it takes to implement these truths and teachings into our lives and make a difference in our world. Think twice before you react to something in a negative way. However, you have to allow yourself to start where you are! If you are hateful then make the positive choice to bring yourself to anger! There is always a higher vibrational place than where you are, when you are in the lower emotions! Let's work on it together so that we can support each other through the shifts and changes!

Channeling Through Susan: As we speak here, we are going to share with you first that is our intention to provide wisdom that will ease the pain that some of you feel. This process of opening the heart and allowing for your true Divinity to be more present with you, can sometimes be arduous for you! We know this and are continually working with you to assist in any way that we can. We will remind you again to request our assistance and guidance and as you do, allow it to flow to you in every way! By this we mean, let go of your expectation of how it should appear and lets us bring it forward in every way possible! Of course in your physical world there are many ways for that to occur! We are wanting to be clear here because we feel that there are many who look past what is being given as divine assistance and love because they are expectant of a different outcome! We are able to assist in ways that you cannot imagine from the limited perspective that you have of the whole! So we ask you to be open and enjoy the beauty that we bring forth to you through your physical world. There is the beauty and the magick in the unfoldment of heaven upon earth! As you request our assistance and presences in your lives you are interacting in a way that allows for us to interact with you through the physical plane, thus bringing heaven upon earth! As above, so below, all around and within! As you allow for the higher vibrational choices to occur through your physical body you are becoming heaven upon earth and co-creating what is meant to be! We are always excited to speak about the ancient wisdom of unconditional love! All that has been shared in these writings is for the purpose of becoming an unconditionally loving people; this is what you have incarnated at this time frame to choose! Use your free will choices as the gift that it is and co-create together a peaceful loving world. We are all one with each other and there is Light in everything! Blessings to you all as you journey and know that we are with you! We love you so much!

Identify the Issue...
Focus on the Solution

So let's get to work! We have very diverse lives with many different circumstances that all create our existence. What we want to focus on is one basic construct that we can take to every circumstance!

1. Start by identifying the "issue"!

2. Redefine "issue": it's an opportunity to interact & choose to make a change that serves your highest good!

3. Take an honest look at where you're feeling place is with regard to the circumstance and explore it enough to feel it.

4. Commit to bringing continual positive change to the circumstance through your thoughts, words, behaviors, feelings and actions.

5. Commit to taking responsibility for your part in the circumstances, being honest, being respectful, being grateful, and working toward forgiveness through your interactions and communications. (Only interact and communicate if you are safe in doing so. Your safety is always the most

important. You integrate respect for yourself through your choice to be safe!)

6. Focus on a solution that will allow you to move forward from the circumstance in a way that serves your highest good and the highest good of all those involved!

7. Communicate, speaking and listening/hearing, with all those involved in the circumstance at hand. This is a very important part of the process, especially with those who you have intimate relationships with. (All those who you spend large amounts of time with and those who are significant people in your life)

8. As you communicate through listening/hearing, remember to understand the other person's perspective and know that what they are sharing is important to them.

9. As you communicate through speaking, remember to share from your perspective, what it is like for you rather than what the other person is doing to you. (EX. "I felt angry when I heard what you said to me and I deserve more respect than that." Rather than: "you made me really angry when you said what you said to me. You disrespected me and it ruined my whole day, you're a ……..!"

10. Focus on the solution more than the issue and accept an apology when it is given, knowing that the apology means that the solution will be implemented. I would appreciate if from now on you would speak to me with more respect than that. I accept your apology!

11. Leave the resolved past issues in the past where they belong, remain present in the present moment. In other words don't continue to bring up something that has already been resolved if it's not reoccurring and remember that some things take a little while to change, so remain focused on the solution!

12. Commit to tell yourself a different story about anything that you have resentment toward so that you can give and receive forgiveness.

It may be helpful for you to write the issues and the solutions. Journaling is always a wonderful way to release and let go as you are able to see exactly where you are in your own words! It is also very helpful to write down how many things you're grateful for at the end of every day! Remember where your attention goes, your energy flows, so choose wisely what you pay attention to through your thoughts, words, behaviors, feelings, and actions.

Remember to be truthful, take responsibility, respectful, grateful, start from where you are, Communicate, interact, discern, and love!

Live In The Light

Choose It - Become It - Enjoy It - Love It

This is your life, choose to be the Spirit in Human form that you're capable of. Discover the gifts that you have that make your heart sing! If it makes your heart sing, it will bring joy to others as well. We are meant to enjoy our journey here, even though there are circumstances that may involve pain, in the definition that we know it as. Our physical bodies are our temples and we hold our most precious gifts within. Within us are the seeds that allow us to open our hearts and become all that we have come here to be!

Use your free will choice to become a beautiful Spirit in Human form, through your thoughts, words, behaviors, feelings and actions. As you choose it, you become it and begin to see the fruits of your labor. Remember that you are part of all that is and that there is much more than meets the eye in the physical world that you live in. Have the faith to know that your choices to become the pure positive and divine Spirit that you are will allow for your Human form to blossom. Even when it seems that you're not seeing results of your actions in your life experience, know that they're on their way! If not for you, for future generations!

Enjoy the beauty of the changes that you are a part of! Make the choice to enjoy all of the little things that once passed you by as you were preoccupied with denser vibrational emotions and choices! There are always gifts that we can find even in the midst of turmoil. Enjoy the breaths you take that allow for more relaxation and peace to enter your life. Enjoy through the healing energy of laughter! Choose to Live in the Light. Blessings Susan

Thank you

I would like to take this opportunity to thank Spirit for the gifts and opportunities that I have been able to experience through my life! It is my hope that this workbook will add to the many writings already in our world that assist people in opening their hearts! My life circumstances have allowed me to experience many different things that have provided opportunities for unconditional love and compassion to be present in my life! I am so grateful for all of the support that I have always had, even when it felt as though I was very alone in the world. I am still learning and growing and even more excited to be a part of the bright future that is unfolding in front of my eyes! The truth and wisdom that I've been hearing from Spirit for the last 10 years, has become a passion. I feel honored and privileged to share it in this way, as well as through living it through my choices in everyday life! I wish for everyone to take the opportunities in their lives and interact with them in unconditionally loving ways! Enjoy the process of re-uniting with the unconditional love that exists within every one of us and use it as you live your life. Share it with yourself and others and all that is, it's the only choice that makes sense! I have included some of the wisdom that I have received through written channeling from Spirit through the years to give you a feel for what I have experienced. These are examples of the teachings of truth and wisdom that I received as I was journeying through my life circumstances. Often in the morning I would be awakened with a sentence of thoughts running through my mind. I would get up and begin to write and as soon as I set the pen onto the paper, the rest would flow through me!

Live Laugh Love Forgive and be Grateful!
From My Heart Susan

Additional Channelings

Divine Unions

It is your ability to see beyond the darkness by allowing, receiving, knowing and being the Light, Power and Love. It is the union of integrated spiritual beings within the fabric that bring the Light forward and assist and enable the ascension process! The union of two spiritual/earthbound beings is the ultimate Light, Power and Love in Action. These couples have integrated themselves with spirit and thus opened to the union with their twin flame or split being and raise to the next levels of consciousness rapidly. This rapid ascension facilitates others' ascensions and provides a strength that they've not experienced in this lifetime on earth! The strength of the union/partnership is a bond that directly affects energy and we (The One, spirit guides, etc.) guide and support you as you move forward into uncharted territory for your spiritually integrated ego/mind! We know that it is courageous as you don't have memory of all that is! We assure you that all that you can perceive both "good and bad" are illusions and that these perceptions will continue to change and expand as you move forward with our guidance.

Choices

Listen to your earthly body and its vibrations and choose accordingly from love and commitment to spirit and your higher self. It is on all fronts that your become balanced and at peace with Mother Earth and Spirit. Your life path on earth gives you opportunities to experience all things in love, peach and gratitude through the Light, Power and Love. Health, relationships, prosperity, education, spirituality, etc. they are all within the circle of life on earth and all contribute to your spiritual integration and thus ascension. Move forward with spirit (love) and walk away from ego (fear) that restricts you!

Action

Believe what you feel and act on it. Your feeling when generated from Light, Power and Love are pure and are divine truth. These are things that ego learns from when spirit has the strength and courage to live in faith and integrity.

Abundance

The $ is here for you as you know it is. Part of the human journey is trusting and having faith in what you know in spite of the lack of its' physical existence. The more you know you have, even though it doesn't appear that you do, the closer it is to manifesting. Then one minute it's there and your path has forever changed and elevated to you divine worthiness and fulfillment!

The Seven Directions

The seven directions are very important for the healing and progression of Mother Earth and her ascension. As you master the use of the seven directions, the directional focus of the colors that are initiated as a result, combined with the intensity of your vibrations combined YOU become a strength and power that is unchallenged. This powerful healing tool is so strong because it is grounded in Mother Earth, illuminated in spirit and supported and enveloped by the elements that make up the earth bound *energy. This energy, in the earth bound plane, can be directed and used for the highest good in which the knowledge of the four elements combined with Light, Power and Love are united. These seven directions are the circle of healing and are an integral force in the ascension of Mother Earth. The two of you are powerful Masters/Magick-ians and have done much loving work in the past. It is now time for you to remember and bring them into the present consciousness. You have proven your strength, commitment and love many times over and are embarking on a very important journey. The combination of your willingness to remember, your openness to things unimaginable and your commitment to universe & self & each other is why you are on this journey together. We are with you always and are proud and grateful for your deep love of all things.*

Remembering

As you seek to find the answers to your questions, you will remember the ancient truths that you once know and lived before entering your earthly bodies this life time. As you remember the excitement and gratitude, they will propel you further and further forward and the truth will be so apparent and visible that you will know from within what your path is! As you, as you call it…leapfrog, it is a collective and inspired journey that is going to provide healing and awareness on many levels!

In Sedona, there will be a culmination of energies and divinity tools that we are assisting in your remembering them. The difference between you and many others, is that not only do you listen to what we share with you, you put it to USE. All that you are receiving and acting on is divine guidance and your power is escalating. You shall find all that you seek and all that you seek we shall give you in one form or another. Your connection to the one is, in essence, your own wisdom and your divine piece of knowledge that you've always had within you. We await each human's awakening and for their reconnection of spirit despite the hold of the earthbound ego. Once that reconnection occurs, all will be revealed as you are ready and as is necessary. The power has always been there for the taking and it is such power that in order to reconnect one has to be of the Light, Power and Love! Such power misused can be detrimental to The One and its' evolution. There are a small percentage of incarnate masters who have listened within open hearts as you have done thus far. It is the power that you possess of the split "being" brought to a place of "being" whole once again that has escalated your evolution and positioning to assist in this very important task at hand. The energy is powerful and filled with Love.

Diamond Light Portals

The seven directions and the healing colors with the collection of energy are powerful. The strength when directed and focused into the diamond, as you refer to it, is more than you can imagine! It is filled with the angelic realm and the inner realm when called upon that way. The spectrum of light which illuminates in physical terms also illuminates the dark beings. Whether or not they want to step forward into the light and walk with the light is their choice, but they aren't able to overcome the Light! No matter what shows they put on and there may/will be some good efforts on their part to detour your efforts, the Light, Power and Love with the seven directions stands firm and strong. Know this!!!!!!

Crystalline Flower

The crystalline flower that you now possess is a gift from The One to you. This is a gift of gratitude for you faith, commitment and love for yourselves, one another and The One in your pursuit of fulfilling your life purpose. Your knowing and awareness of the process that is at hand has enabled you to open gateways that will allow the circle to be complete once again! It is within that circle that everything is reunited and is able to move forward. It is the conscious choice in physical form that allows the collective consciousness to rise. It is your awareness of the importance of the process that is allowing universe to assist you as you provide and share your gifts to The One and that will assist in bringing the circle back to its' place of origin! Yes it is golden and yes it has everything to do with unconditional universal love. The crystalline flower was one of many that were physical manifestations of the times of Lemuria and

Atlantis and represented just how pure and strong unconditional love and gratitude really are and the peace within that came as a result of it. We have gifted you with this magickal flower and the love that you are remembering with a "True Love" partner is what activates the mystical and magickal power of the crystalline flower!

Magick Withing Us All

It truly is the magick within us all that allows the magick of the ancient wisdom to resurface and become what it once was and yearns to be again! It has been an arduous process for those who were in Lemuria and Atlantis and a courageous journey with many teachings along the way. We are succeeding and the time has come to reunite with our pure divinity. The divinity that is our birthright, our destiny and what was intended from day one. "True Love Unions" "Sacred Unions" will continue to grow rapidly, with love, strength, respect, trust, joy, peace and gratitude. The more they grow the more power and ability to make use of the crystal you will have! We will guide you through the process and you will enjoy all of our communications with you! We will always be sure that you "know' what to do, when to do it and how to go about it. Have faith, pay attention, use the bond that the "sacred Unions" have together and the gifts that both bring to the partnership to assist you as you journey on the path.

The strength of the union propels you into the wisdom of the ages! We are enjoying this process as much as you are and it is an exciting time as we can see our many years of work coming to a place of fruition! There are many pieces to this puzzle and it is being closely observed by all areas of the Galactic Omnipresent vibration. Listen to any and all information that you are receiving and continue to discern what is best for each of the union to do! You are setting an example for the physical to emulate! The people looking from the outside will be amazed and inspired by the love, joy, fun and commitment that you exude. Relax and enjoy your process together. We love you. The One

Vibrations

Your vibrations are going to be very high when you go to Peru. Much higher than it is now!! Everything that you are doing, spiritually and earthly, is raising your awareness and your vibration in preparation for what is to come. Each divine union is being asked to remember what they contracted to do!! This includes rituals, activations, initiations, symbols and commitments done from love and faith both earthly and spiritually. We are with you every step of the way. We are guiding and giving you everything that you need. Continue to open to yourself, each other and spirit. As you open to all that is here for you, you will receive more of the peace and gratitude that you love allows! Love is the source of all that is. Love is The One, You are The One! It all is The One!! The expanded awareness that is necessary for BE-ing The One is achieved through the process of the expansion of your awareness. Your awareness is expanded by your ability to BE open to all and having faith in all that you receive.

If it seems as though we speak to you in circles….We do!! Everything is about choosing to come full circle and it is all connected. When we speak of The One, we truly, in every sense of the word, want you to understand that it is "ALL" The One! The earthbound spiritual beings that you are have the key to the expansion. Expansion means bringing heaven on earth by the process of you conscious loving choices. The more you can teach by example, the more others will embrace what you are verbally teaching through writing and speaking. Earthbound spirits need visual examples to give them tangible references for what they can emulate and aspire to BE! Therefore, not only are you doing a wonderful job of being open to all we are giving you to do in spiritual work and healing, you are also doing a wonderful job of following your hearts in your earthbound bodies. You teach, heal and learn on all levels that moves you, others and the collective consciousness closer and closer to The One!

As you travel, you will be guided to many different vortices, locations and spiritual experiences that you will be able to choose to listen and act on what spirit is asking through your ability to BE the Light, Power and Love! People will also be brought into your path that your vibration will affect and your divine purity of love and commitment will teach. Just your presence is a portal that people may choose to enter into! They won't understand what or why they are feeling it, but will be able to choose whether or not to integrate those feelings into their life. As you move forward with your journey, your integration will expand rapidly.

There will be things that appear to be of the "dark", but always know it is an illusion and the dark has contracted from a place of light and of course is still the light within. We know you know this, but it is imperative that it is engrained in your human mind so that Light, Power and Love will always be in the forefront and in a place of power. You will have communications with many different vibrations from many different dimensions and all will serve The One by assisting you in coming full circle. The simplicity of the journey, the process and the outcome is too complex for earthbound beings to embrace. It is only when they relinquish control that they become one with spirit again. It really is simple and easy when looked upon in this way. You are able to translate this simplicity through your love, divine and sacred union, humor and example of commitment to self, each other and spirit! Enjoy and have fun!

Ease

Dear Ones, you have done a large amount of spiritual and earthly work in a short period of time! You have brought your earthbound spirit vibrations to a place in which you can move in all directions freely. We are pleased with your accomplishments and are excited that you are aware and grateful for the work you have done. Now that you know and understand the love of The One, you are going to move forward on your path together with ease. This journey is filled with love, joy, peace and gratitude and will serve the highest good as you move forward with the strength and power of the Light, Power and Love!

We are always here to answer any questions you might have or give support and/or confirmation on any subject or circumstance. You both have gracefully and elegantly moved into the life purpose and life path that you contracted for and as you move forward together, you will gain the strength and speed that is necessary for the job at hand. The love of self, each other and The One is in place and activated and will only continue to expand as we guide you forward on the journey. The details of what you are to experience and contribute will unfold with ease. The circumstances around you will be easy to discern. All you need to concern yourself with is what serves yourselves, which in turn serves the highest good.

Continue to work with your power, magick, spiritual abilities and as you practice these gifts will expand. The time of expansion (heaven on earth) is upon us and some of you have come to this realization ahead of the rest of the pack! This is in divine and perfect order and is necessary for the ascension process. As you, on the leading edge, are raising the vibration for Mother Earth, she will move forward as well. Focus on the gifts you've received and use and enjoy them to their fullest with each other. Bless you as we are less than a breath away Always and in All Ways.

See With Your Heart

We want you to know that as you look through your heart as opposed to your eyes, you will see clearly what is reality. Reality is what you know to be true in this moment and Sacred Unions are very clear on what IS and always will be. As you see and live through your heart, in joy, all will fall into place! The world around you will not understand or comprehend how you can remain so steadfast in your commitment to self, spirit and each other in the midst of the turmoil. They will, however, be inspired by the energy that is emitted from your vibration. You will give them hope and a feeling of safety that eases the pain of their fear. Even if they don't outwardly show it, their higher self will embrace it and keep them inwardly grounded! You are truly anchored in yourself and by being anchored to spirit, you have allowed your reunion which has amplified all that you feel and do! The strength and purity of the partnership is what is needed at this time and will continue to grow. What you are experiencing in your sleep states are often so deep that you will not remember. We are working with you and you with us every time you rest your physical body. Spirit is The One that is teaching you and assisting you as you move forward. You will and are more receptive to everything around you as a result of the work that we do with you. You have a team of The One always with you as you are divine and vibrating at a rate that is fast now.

Health---The Master Of Your Choices

As you exercise, the self control of your diet and health of your body, you are training yourself to have control of the universal powers at hand! Your higher conscious mind is directly connected to spirit and has an open line of communication to your conscious mind to the degree that you allow it. It is important to make significant strides in your progress of becoming spiritually integrated and in harmony with yourselves and each other. As you master control over your choices and follow the info being downloaded to you, you enable magick within and the power it holds. By doing this, your awareness is raised and you life path is ever moving in the perfect and divine direction!

Feeling Drained?

As you move through your days, the journey may leave you feeling drained. We have listened to you discussing this and wondered why you haven't asked for our help. You are accurate in the thoughts of the higher energies causing discord between the lower vibrations of the body. This will continue on and off as the Sacred Unions are moving forward rapidly with the increase of awareness and higher conscious energy flow. You may ask for our assistance at any time and we will help you with this. You must request it though because we are bound by divine contract to serve you and that requires you to consciously request our assistance and we will give it!! Many don't realize this and wonder why spirit has forsaken them. We were ready and willing, but unable to cross the boundary of human existence because our help wasn't requested. We enjoy assisting you in your evolution as this is our life path. It is our life path to journey in harmony along side of you as a team. We love our job and never tire of the work or the joy we receive through your joy of evolving.

Gifts

We wanted to share more with you about the gifts in the boxes and the significance of them and their timing. You are able to see how closely connected Sacred Unions are through your progress and growth. We are so pleased and just as excited that you choose to receive us, to hear us and to KNOW.

What we are wanting to tell you is that with in a Sacred Union, both individuals bring different parts to the whole. You are alike in so many ways and share qualities that set you apart from many. Your vibration is high and your integrity, devotion, love and commitment are why you are where you are. You also have dissimilar qualities that compliment each other. I know we have discussed this before and explained it in many ways. To recap, the earthbound journey requires teamwork, partnership, remembering and reunion and what you are to choose to come full circle with. The self and spirit reunion must first occur before the reunion with your split being. In essence, you are all split beings because you are all part of The One! But, what we're referring to are two vibrational spirits in human form that were born of one vibration to begin with. As you descend into human form, you each follow the path of your life purpose which inevitably leads you back to your divine partner. In order to live your life paths together, there have to be specialties that you both/each excel at and compliment the pair with. It is only when you have come into re-union with your higher self, spirit, The One that you are able to accept, respect, honor, support, love and EMBRACE your complimentary integrated spiritual partner...your divine partner that you were once one with. The joy of these reunions are euphoric and unlike anything imaginable on earth. The qualities that you each have that define you and allow you to, so successfully work together are directly related to the male/masculine and female/feminine roles on earth. Just like any other partnership, there are strengths and weaknesses in both. There are ALL qualities in each of you, but the purity of love allows each of those qualities to excel in ALL areas just as they are supposed to. Where one leaves off the other picks up! It is an harmonic dance of love, trust, acceptance, respect, honor, gratitude and peace! The commitment between the two of you is the strongest, most powerful bond that exists in vibration because you truly feel what it is like to be One/ The One! It is The One in human form and emulates in all ways the highest energy in existence! The Light, Power and Love that emanates from you is a life altering form of energy with a driving force from the two of you to share it in any way that you can for the highest good. We know you are enjoying this process as much as we are! We know that this explanation of your vibrations will resonate with you, as well.

Contentment And Nourishment

There is a great need for contentment in our vibrational field. With contentment and as contentment is achieved, the vibration of peace, love and gratitude will be accessed. The sickly and ravished cat that came to your worksite and was given attention has shown you how people exist with little or no nourishment and although they appear to be beyond reaching and or changing they always are. The dis-ease, dis-comfort, dis-asters, dis-enchantment, dis-cord, etc. that they experience and feel are only temporary as they can change direction at any given moment in time. They can feel the relief of peace, love and gratitude and thus contentment of where they are on their path. The cat, despite its' appearance today is feeling contentment and peace because it has received love which is nourishment, as well as physical nourishment. IT KNOWS its' safe and will continue moving forward from here. This holds true not only for people, but for the land, the vibration of the land and anything that is alive! This concept is what you are providing for people. You are providing nourishment for their spiritual vibration and nourishment for their physical bodies with the universal knowledge, experiences and love that allow them to see, feel and experience what IS possible and easily accessible to them.

As you have learned, to discern what serves you, you learn what serves The One! By serving The One consciously, you are raising the collective consciousness of the whole. Bringing harmony into the vibrational field everywhere you go. The class last night was divine and had a large impact, as well as causing a shift in all who attended. The vibration of the space is also raised and enhanced with each interaction you have with it. Yes, we mean that you interact with your surroundings as the two of you consciously share the gift of the divine union everywhere you interact together. The combination of your energies, which unite as ONE and is very powerful, are energizing the fabric in a divine, pure and guided way. We would love for you to know the ease that flows from the two of you as you teach and share. We know you are feeling it.

You will both be experiencing new and amazing feelings, openings, peace as you continue to walk forward on the path of enlightenment and harmony. This is why the two of you are being asked to work together in all circumstances, although it doesn't feel like work to you! We know the gratitude and love that you feel as you serve The One and follow our guidance which is actually your guidance that we assist you with. The amped energy is now being taken into Susan's work and locations that we want to benefit from the love of The One that emits from your union.

Each location you encounter, each and every person you interact with benefits them on many levels and is providing opportunities to love themselves through the exposure to new references that have never been shown to them before. To touch the lives and vibrations of all those you encounter is how you nourish and bless The One. Nourishing all with love is the most wonderful gift there is to give. For once it's received, a shift is made that allows for all to proceed forward with the Light, Power and Love! We will talk with you often about your earthly ways of sharing through your classes, website, teachings and life coaching. Namaste

Focus

We want you to know that as you focus on what you're doing with your physical body through meticulous tasks and artistry, you increase your ability to draw upon the universal energies that you have access to. You have said it to many, Susan, you thought your work has allowed you to open to receiving from us. So it is and will continue in many other *ways for you. It is through your focus on your health, your exercise, diet, spiritual awareness, paying attention, work with current jobs, work with upcoming career paths, classes, etc. ALL that you DO! Your direction is fueled by the focus you put into it. All of the life exercises you are living, breathing, being and doing right now are all enhancing your abilities to focus. Your focus, the ability to focus, is a direct channel to your power.*

We told you we would be guiding you in many areas and training/teaching you in ways that would empower you. This is yet another important piece of your circle. You are in apprenticeship with spirit right now and are learning the skill sets required for you to move forward with ease. These were all planned and contracted with your presence and input and are now simply being acted out and put into practice. We are hitting in all areas of your life it is important for you to be easy on yourselves as you learn and ascend. Focus is a strength exercise that allows you the power to access your divine powers. In accessing your divine powers, you move forward with ease!

We are wanting to clarify "divine powers" for you. We don't mean witch like powers, we mean earthbound spiritual powers to focus, discern, have the ability to observe us, make choices without fear and attachment and to have integrity. To LIVE in love in all you do and to be open to receiving all and giving all you receive. We mean by powers, your strength of spirit in an earthbound physical body. It is your power to live in spirit, with spirits sight, in spirits time and make use of spirit in all earthly ways. This is the magick and the gift that you have to enjoy and give because most cave in and crumble under expectation and judgment and rules that fit a construct that is an earthly reality. Earthly reality is what restricts people from remembering what The One and the love of The One really is! The divine and sacred unions are her to lovingly prove by example otherwise. Giving people new and unbelievable references to draw on as they yearn to remember and open. You see, they are all beginning to feel unsettled with earthbound realities. Each soul is beginning to question what is going on around them. It doesn't quite feel right to them anymore. This is due to the collective consciousness being higher than ever before. It changes the cellular structure of The One. As the cellular structure changes, it opens to new examples of love and joy in spite of what has been their experience! Again, dear ones, you are nourishing the whole with your examples of commitment, contentment, focus, love and actions for yourself, The One and each other. You are a living, breathing example of the wholly/holy trinity and the love, joy and gratitude that accompany it.

Can This Be?

We hear you Susan that it's unbelievable that these channelings are what they are and yet also knowing that they "are" what they are and allowing them even though it doesn't make earthly sense. If you knew for sure that it was what it is you wouldn't have to make the conscious choice to allow it, act on it, believe it and know it!!! Most importantly BE IT!!! This is the path. It is the process by which you contracted and agreed to teach, share and serve The One! It is the only way to raise the collective consciousness and allow Mother Earth to come into her full Goddess loving power and for the universe to benefit from the ascension of all. Do you see? We know you do as it is clear to you as you experience it.

Focus And Intention

The combination of focus and intention allows the Light, Power and Love to come through in an enormous way. Focus without intention has less power and wastes your abilities to share your gifts. Intention without focus is a waste of power. As you proceed through the process of raising your awareness, your ability to focus increases and intention becomes stronger. In the past, there were beings that used their focus that was not for a divine purpose. In these situations, the power is misused. Use your focus and intention in a loving way and your power and awareness will increase. These activations and understandings will assist Sacred Unions in moving forward as a team. Always the polarities.... The team of two individuals, the team of individuals in spirit...Inspired.

What Can We Change?

We know you are wondering how it all works and what you have the power to change. These are complex questions that have clear answers, but they're complex answers as well. As there are many layers to refer to in your existence. It is very expanded and it seems as though your inner knowing sometimes remembers many things from your past spiritual history. What we are wanting you to know is that as we have acknowledged before that "yes" anything is possible, "yes" everything is here for you and "yes" you can change anything in spiritual terms. These answers all have different levels of awareness that dictate to what degree you are capable of bringing them into being. Earth is a place that has boundaries, so to speak, when you are in an earthbound form. Bringing spirit into the earthbound form expands what you can achieve, as well as, what you draw to you in your experience! Although you are The One and technically capable of All That Is, you have contracted and chosen to inhabit an earthbound body with earthbound vibrations and limitations. There are certain limitations on earth and these limitations are divinely imposed so that the process can move forward of consciously choosing to move beyond these limitations.

We will speak of polarity as on earth as it is a necessary part of existence and this process raises the collective consciousness. Each earthbound body has a path that they contracted to walk and come into alignment with. When they are moving forward on their path, there will be much growth and therefore raising of awareness and their vibration. As with everything, we want you to know that your vibration is where it is because of the work you've done. As you move forward, your vibration will tell you through your abilities to feel where you are at and if it is in harmony or not. As you move forward in one area of your life, the other areas will change as well. This is being in harmony with who you've become. Sometimes it takes a while for your physical surroundings and interactions to come up to speed and this would be tying up loose ends. The dwellings that you both inhabit also change as you change as do your activities and experiences!

Expectation

As you move through your time and space, we provide you with gifts of all forms. Each gift is an opportunity for expansion, meaning spiritual growth! Whether it be animals, numbers, other's channelings, light shows, star miracles, synchronicities, and also seemingly adverse situations through earth eyes (illnesses, death, turmoil, negativity). It is all part of the plan. It is part of your training to learn to embrace all that is as Love and Light. There lies the power. We want you to understand that expectation is an earthbound quality and it is a divine quality, as well, because it allows you to move beyond expectation into knowing through conscious choices in all forms. The greater your capacity to embrace, not only what makes sense and fits what you want, but the experiences that "seem" to be impossible, miraculous, heinous and nonsensical...the greater your awareness and consciousness become!

Expectation limits your ability to embrace and grow spiritually. It is the polarity and oneness of detachment and connectedness that frees you from your human boundaries and allows spirit (The One) BE! This is the ultimate goal on earth, to consciously choose to be who you are remembering you are! Spirit/The One is pure love, it is the light that illuminate All, it is the Love and Light that create your power to choose The One. It is The One that transforms your human existence into expansion, Heaven on Earth! Light, Power, Love...Love, Light, Power...Power, Love, Light, etc. these three qualities are the holy trinity and the qualities of The One! No matter what order you use them in they are one, they work together to achieve The One because they are The One. When you can use these three qualities in harmony with one another you become one with love, purity, divine inception of The One in human form.

There is no greater gift than that of detaching from the human ego consciously and stepping into the power of the Love/Light of The One! By dethatching we do not mean disconnecting. Your ego is an important part of being a spirit on human form. As you detach, you become reconnected to your source of the Love and Light that you are and were always meant to be! It is the ultimate gift and the ultimate sacrifice to get there. As you see, hear and read by our writings, it is all One! There is no separation. As you detach, you leave expectation behind as expectation limits you and your power. We know this is the most difficult part of transforming human to spirit in human form! It is, however, the most rewarding and is what allows you to transmute and feel joy, love and peace unlike anything you could experience through expectation and limitation. The expansion is never ending and those of you who are beginning this ascent; we are elated to share the love with you once again. So as you remember and reconnect, be easy on yourself as you release yourself from expectation and thus detachment. It is meant to be for you have contracted to be the living example of this transformation for those who aren't strong enough to do it on their own. It is the ultimate gift to humanity that those of you on the leading edge are giving! In Love we trust, through Love is The One with Light, Power and Love you become The One and are The One in every minute.

Acknowledgments
My journey of wisdom

These are the incredible authors who have assisted me in my evolutionary process. Thanks to each and every one of you from the bottom of my heart! I have also shared the changes that I have made along the way!

<u>Echo Bodine</u>: Echoes of the Soul, A Still Small Voice, Hands that Heal

<u>Doreen Virtue</u>: Healing with the Angels, Angel Therapy, Devine Guidance, Devine Prescriptions, Angel Numbers, Divine Magic, The Healing Miracles of Arch Angel Raphael, The Miracles of Arch Angel Michael, Angel Words, Healing Words From the Angels, and all card decks

<u>James Redfield</u>: The Celestine Prophecy, Shambala

<u>Deepak Chopra</u>: The Seven Spiritual Laws of Success

<u>Greg Braden</u>: The God Code, Lost Mode of Prayer, The Matrix

<u>Eckhart Tolle</u>: The Power of Now, The New Earth

<u>Louise Hay</u>: Love Yourself, Heal Your Life

<u>Ted Andrews</u>: Animal Speak, Nature-Speak, Animal Wise, Intercesion of Spirits

Dr. Wayne Dyer: You'll See It When You Believe It, There's A Spiritual Solution To Every Problem, Pulling g Your Own Strings, Your Sacred Self, The Power Of Intention Getting In The Gap, The 10 Secrets Of Success And Inner Peace, Meditations for Manifesting

Masarru Emoto: Water Crystal Healing

Neale Donald Walsch: The Little Soul and Sun, The Little Soul and the Earth, Conversations with God (books 1,2,&3)

Esther and Jerry Hicks, Abraham Hicks: The Law of Attraction, Ask and It Is

Given, Living the Art of Allowing, The Vortex

Carolyn M. Sutherland: The Body Knows

Christine Northrop:

Brian Tracey: Eat That Frog

Neville Johnston: Hidden Language Codes

Rhonda Byrne: The Secret

James Arthur Ray: The Science of Success, Practical Spirituality, Collapse The World, Power Transformations.

Stanislave Grof,MD: The Holotropic Mind

Wallace D. Wattles: The Science of getting Rich

David R. Hawkins, MD., Ph.D.: Power VS. Force

Gay and Kathlyn Hendricks: The Relationship Solution (AWESOME!!!!!)

Tom Kenyon and Judi Sian:The magdalin Manuscript James Redfield: The Secret Of Shambala James Redfield

Joe Vitale: Zero Limits

Michael Beckwith: Life Visioning Process

William P. Young: The Shack

Marie Manuchehri: The Seven Primary Chaukras, Embrace Your Intuition

Max Freedom Long: The Secret Science Behind Miracles

Judith Blue Stone Polich: Return of the Children of the Light

Dunvalo Melchizadeck: The Flower of Life

Kathleen Pepper: Hand in Hand with the Angels (One of my all time favorites)

Maureen J. St. Germain: Beyond the Flower of Life

There are still many books on my book shelf that I have yet to read. All of the books above, I have read or listened to over and over again and I highly recommend!!

Seminars and Conferences and Certifications

Abraham Hicks Art of Allowing Work Shop: Cincinnati, Ohio and Orlando, Fla.

I can Do It Conference 2005 Orlando, Fla.: Greg Braden, Wayne Dyer, Esther and Jerry Hicks, Dawn Breslin, Steven Farmer, Doreen Virtue, Christine Northrop, Masaru Emoto

Phoenix Books: Neville Johnston

James Arthur Ray: The Secret of Attracting True Wealth, The Harmonic Wealth Week end, Modern Magic, Practical Mysticism,

Dick Sutphen:The Accelerating Shift in Sedona, arizona 2007

Shelly Stockwell: NLP and Stress Management Practitioner certifications

Bruce Vinikas: Flower of Life Workshop

Dietary, Physical, and Personal changes that I made as I have raised my awareness

Regular Healing Touch and Reiki: Sue Keiser

Regular Spiritual Body Work: Acupressure, Chiropractic, Massage therapy, Reflexology: Phan Wellness Center (Chau Phan and Cuc Phan)

Healthier Eating

Supplements and Noni juice and Amigo Juice

Yoga

Meditation

Stopped watching the news

Watch only 1-2 hours of TV per week, (lately, not even that)

Stopped using disempowering words (don't, try, want, maybe, hopefully, hope, etc.)

Use empowering words for everything (I'm still monitoring closely, every now and then I have to Cancel a slip up!!)

Cleaning off the shelves inside my body of all past negativity that I was storing, by redefining my perceptions of my past "Bad" experiences.

Replace the redefined perceptions with gratitude and love.

Followed my intuition whether I understood it or not

Gave and am still giving any and all information that I receive from my vibration, to the people that God has me cross paths with.

Show gratitude to God and the universal helpers who communicate with me frequently every day through words, numbers, nature, and animals, specifically Hawks!!!

Journaling and writing for me to achieve goal of writing a book and curriculum for seminars and motivational speaking.

Pay attention to any situation that triggers a negative response and immediately begin the process of finding the gift within the situation.

Learned to love myself, by understanding that my fears were an illusion as I tell myself the truth.

Learned to love my body

Ball Room Dance Lessons at Arthur Murray Dance Studio

Learned to be AVAILABLE!!!:)

Consciously choosing to be present in my present moments.

Knowing that it's a life long journey and it's enjoying the journey itself that is leading a life guided by spirit.

Special Support Thank You's

Thank you so much to everyone who contributed financially to publishing this book! I am very grateful to each and every one of you for your love and support!

    Chris Salomone
    Scotia Minarsch
    Carolyn and Bill Christian
    Sherry and Tim Tilesz
    Pearl of Wisdom
    Nicole and Deron Klatte
    Jo Ann Kelly
    Kathy Fulop
    Terry Ohanlon
    Bonnie Helt

Pearls of Wisdom:
3522 N High St.
Columbus Ohio
614-262-0146

Phoenix Books:
3110 N. High St.
Columbus Oh 43202
614-268-3100